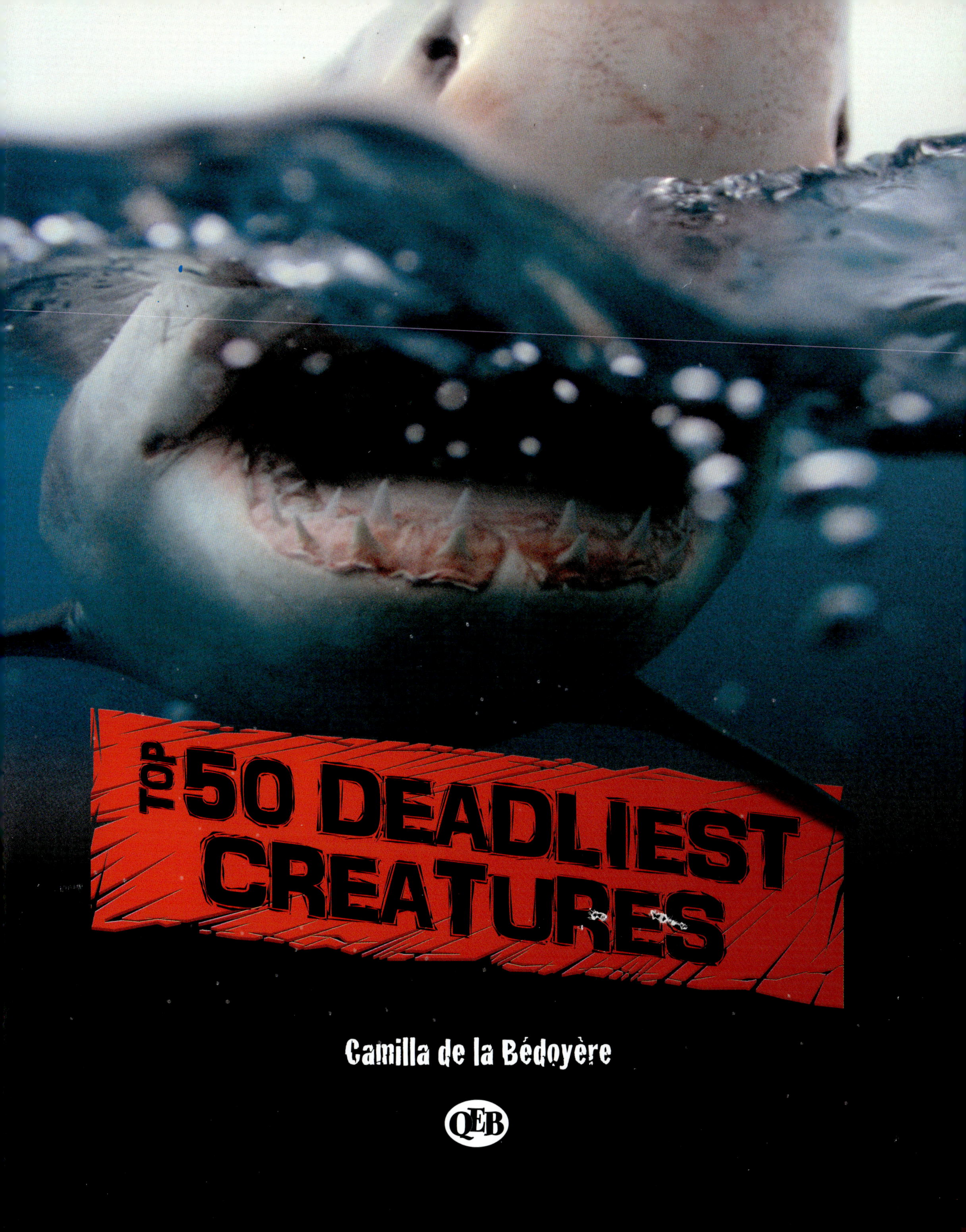

TOP 50 DEADLIEST CREATURES

Camilla de la Bédoyère

QEB

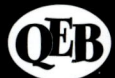

Created for QEB Publishing by Tall Tree Ltd
www.talltreebooks.co.uk
Editors: Jon Richards and Rob Colson
Designer: Jonathan Vipond
Illustration pp18–19:
Mick Posen/www.the-art-agency.co.uk

Copyright © QEB Publishing, Inc. 2012

Published in the United States by
QEB Publishing, Inc.
3 Wrigley, Suite A
Irvine, CA 92618

www.qed-publishing.co.uk

All rights reserved. No part of this publication may be reproduced, stored in a retrieval system, or transmitted in any form or by any means, electronic, mechanical, photocopying, recording, or otherwise, without the prior permission of the publisher, nor be otherwise circulated in any form of binding or cover other than that in which it is published and without a similar condition being imposed on the subsequent purchaser.

A CIP record for this book is available from the Library of Congress.

ISBN 978 1 60992 285 6

Printed in China

Picture credits
(t=top, b=bottom, l=left, r=right, c=center, fc=front cover, bc=back cover)
Alamy: 8-9 Stephen Frink Collection, 20-21 Mark Conlin, 21br David Fleetham, 26-27 Gerry Pearce, 30 blickwinkel, 30-31 Amazon-images, 2bl William Mullins, 48-49 Wildlife GmbH, 74-75 Alaska Stock, 86-87 Phil Degginger, 91t Allstar Picture Library, 94-95 Naturepix, 104b WaterFrame,110-111 David Fleetham; **Corbis:** 49 DLILLC, 61t Tom Brakefield, 61b Theo Allofs, 66-67 W Perry Conway, 72 Thomas Kitchin & Victoria Hurst/All Canada Photos, 106-107 ML Sinibaldi; **Creative Commons:** 44bl Bjorn Christian Torrissen; **Dreamstime:** 50bl Yaireibovich; **FLPA** 17tr Malcolm Schuyl, 39t D P Wilson, 42-43 Thomas Marent, 43t Thomas Marent, 51br Peter Davey, 70bl Piotr Naskrecki, 70-71 Chien Lee, 78-79 Norbert Wu/Minden Pictures, 81b Reinhard Dirscherl, 80-81 Norbert Wu/Minden Pictures, 84bl Hiroya Minakuchi/Minden Pictures, 96-97 Pete Oxford/Minden Pictures ,114 Mike Parry/Minden Pictures
Getty Images: 12 Visuals Unlimited, 23 Mark Moffett, Inc./Michael Kern, 40 Mark Moffett, 41r Visuals Unlimited, Inc/Alex Wild, 60 Vivek Sinha,64-65 Pete Oxford, 72-73 Robert Postma, 74af Daniel J Cox, 75br Altrendo Nature, 86bl James H Robinson, 95t Dorling Kindersley, 110-111 AFP; **Minibeast Wildlife:** 82bl Alan Henderson; **Nature Picture Library:** 4-5 Alex Mustard, 6b Alan James, 13t Michael D Kern, 16-17 Joe McDonald, 17b Doug Perrine, 18-19 Doug Perrine, 19t Dan Burton, 20b Alan James, 30-31 Doug Perrine, 36-37 Alex Mustard, 37t David Fleetham, 38-39 Doug Perrine, 46-47 Doug Perrine, 47t Dan Burton, 55b Michael D. Kern, 71 Rod Williams, 74-75 Alex Mustard , 75t David Fleetham, 79t Alex Hyde, 85t Alex Hyde, 91t Barry Mansell, 103b Doug Perrine, 104-105 Jeff Rotman, 107br Inaki Relanzon, 108-109 Jeff Rotman, 109r Andy Rouse, 112-113 Martin Dohrn; **NHPA** 7t Charles Hood, 10bl ANT Photo Library, 14-15 T Kitchen & V Hurst, 15t Image Quest 3D, 19b Daniel Hueclin, 27t Woodfall/Photoshot, 34b, 34-35 Burt Jones and Maurine Shimlock, 40-41 Dave Pinson, 44-45 ANT Photo Library, 45b Ken Griffiths, 50-51 Nick Garbutt, 54 E Hanumantha Rao, 56b, 56-57 Charles Hood, 58-59 Larry Ditto, 64b Martin Wendler, 83 Ken Griffiths, 84-85 Gerard Lacz, 88-89 Ken Griffiths, 89 Photoshot, 90 Mark Conlin, 95b John Bell, 97b Daniel Heuclin, 98-99 Daniel Heuclin, 99b Stephen Dalton, 107t Martin Harvey, 108 Jordi Bas Casasj 111 Martin Harvey, 115t Oceans Image/Photoshot/Saul Gonor; **SPL:** 7b Gerald and Buff Corsi, Visuals Unlimited, Inc., 18-19 Tom McHugh, 19t Merlin Tuttle/Bat Conservation International, 22 Sinclair Stammers, 28-29 Matthew Oldfield, 29b WK Fletcher, 31t Visuals Unlimited, 32-33 Solvin Zankl, 33b Theirry Berrod, Mona Lisa Production, 53b Steve Gschmeissner, 59 Ken M Highfill, 67b Nature's Images, 68b Simon D Pollard, 68-69 Barbara Strnadova, 69c James H Robinson, 76br Steve Gschmeissner, 76-77 Nature's Images, 80b Geoff Kidd, 100t Andy Murch, Visuals Unlimited, Inc., 111t Andy Murch/Visuals Unlimited, Inc., 111b Georgette Douwma, 112bl Susumu Nishinaga,115b Andy Murch/Visuals Unlimited, Inc., 109l John Shaw

Website information is correct at time of going to press. However, the publishers cannot accept liability for any information or links found on any Internet sites, including third-party websites.

Look out for this rating. It will tell you how scary each reptile is.

Words in **bold** are explained in the Glossary on page 122.

1—a little scary
2—pretty scary
3—scary
4—QUICK! RUN AWAY!
5—YIKES! TOO LATE!

CONTENTS

BASKING SHARK 6
LONGNOSE SAWSHARK 8
SCUTIGERA 10
GILA MONSTER 12
ALLIGATOR SNAPPING TURTLE 14
SECRETARY BIRD 16
VAMPIRE BAT 18
ELECTRIC EEL 20
ARMY ANT 22
ARMY ANT 24
TASMANIAN DEVIL 26
SEA SNAKE 28
PIRANHA 30
KILLER BEE 32
DEADLY SHARKS 34
LEMON SHARK 36
EGGS AND PUPS 38
JUMPER ANT 40
LONOMIA 42
PARALYSIS TICK 44
GREY REEF SHARK 46
CHIMPANZEE 48
HONEY BADGER 50
KOMODO DRAGON 52
KING COBRA 54
MAMBA 55
HAMMERHEAD SHARK 56
CORAL SNAKE 58
TIGER 60
TIGER 62
ANACONDA 64
BLACK CAIMAN 66
BIRD-EATING SPIDER 68
ASSASSIN BUG 70
WOLVERINE 72
WOLF 74
BLACK WIDOW SPIDER 76
SKELETONS AND SCALES 78
TIGER SHARK 80
FUNNEL-WEB SPIDER 82
KILLER WHALE 84
BROWN RECLUSE SPIDER 86
TAIPAN 88
ALLIGATOR 90
ALLIGATOR 92
IMPERIAL SCORPION 94
EMPEROR SCORPION AND
DEATH STALKER 95
RATTLESNAKE 96
PUFF ADDER 98
ON THE MOVE 100
BULL SHARK 102
SHARKS AND PEOPLE 104
LION 106
POLAR BEAR 108
SALTWATER CROCODILE 110
MOSQUITO 112
GREAT WHITE SHARK 114
GREAT WHITE SHARK 116
TOP 20 FACTS 118
TAKING IT FURTHER 120
GLOSSARY 122
INDEX 126

Actual size!
Actual size!
Actual size!

Check out this Lemon Shark on page 36

BASKING SHARK

DEADLY BITES

Length: Up to 39 ft (1,200 cm)

Habitat: Coasts and deep oceans

Where: Worldwide

Weapons: A VERY large mouth and sieve-like plates

HOW SCARY?

50 The enormous mouth of a basking shark is large enough to hold a child. Fortunately, a basking shark has no interest in human **prey** because it only eats tiny **plankton**!

The largest basking sharks weigh up to 21 tons (19 tonnes), five times as much as an elephant.

Water and plankton gush into the shark's huge gaping mouth.

Water passes out through the gill slits but the plankton is caught in the gills.

The huge slits on the side of a basking shark's head are called gill slits. Fish use **gills** instead of lungs to breathe underwater. Water, which contains oxygen, passes into their mouth and out through the gills. Basking sharks also use their gills to feed. Sieve-like plates in the gills trap any plankton in the water.

Actual size!

Plankton
Up to 3.2 in (8 cm)

Mystery Shark

Sharks are mysterious creatures, and scientists need to find out much more about their lifestyles. It is known that basking sharks go on long journeys in spring and summer, but no one knows for sure where they disappear to from November to March.

Killer Fact

Basking sharks often swim near the surface of the sea, and can even leap out of the water!

LONGNOSE SAWSHARK

49 This small shark has a peculiar snout that makes up more than one quarter of its whole body length. The shark uses its strange nose, called a rostrum, as a lethal weapon and to detect prey.

The sides of the long nose are lined with rows of teeth.

Up to 17.6 in (45 cm)

Sawsharks have a small, flat body because they live on the seabed and swim close to the bottom, where they hunt for small fish, squid, and shrimp. Their long nose is called a saw and is lined with long, sharp teeth. Long feelers on the saw, called barbels, are used for touch. They also have teeth in their jaws, which they use for biting.

As they cruise along the seabed, sawsharks use their barbels to detect prey hidden in the sand and mud.

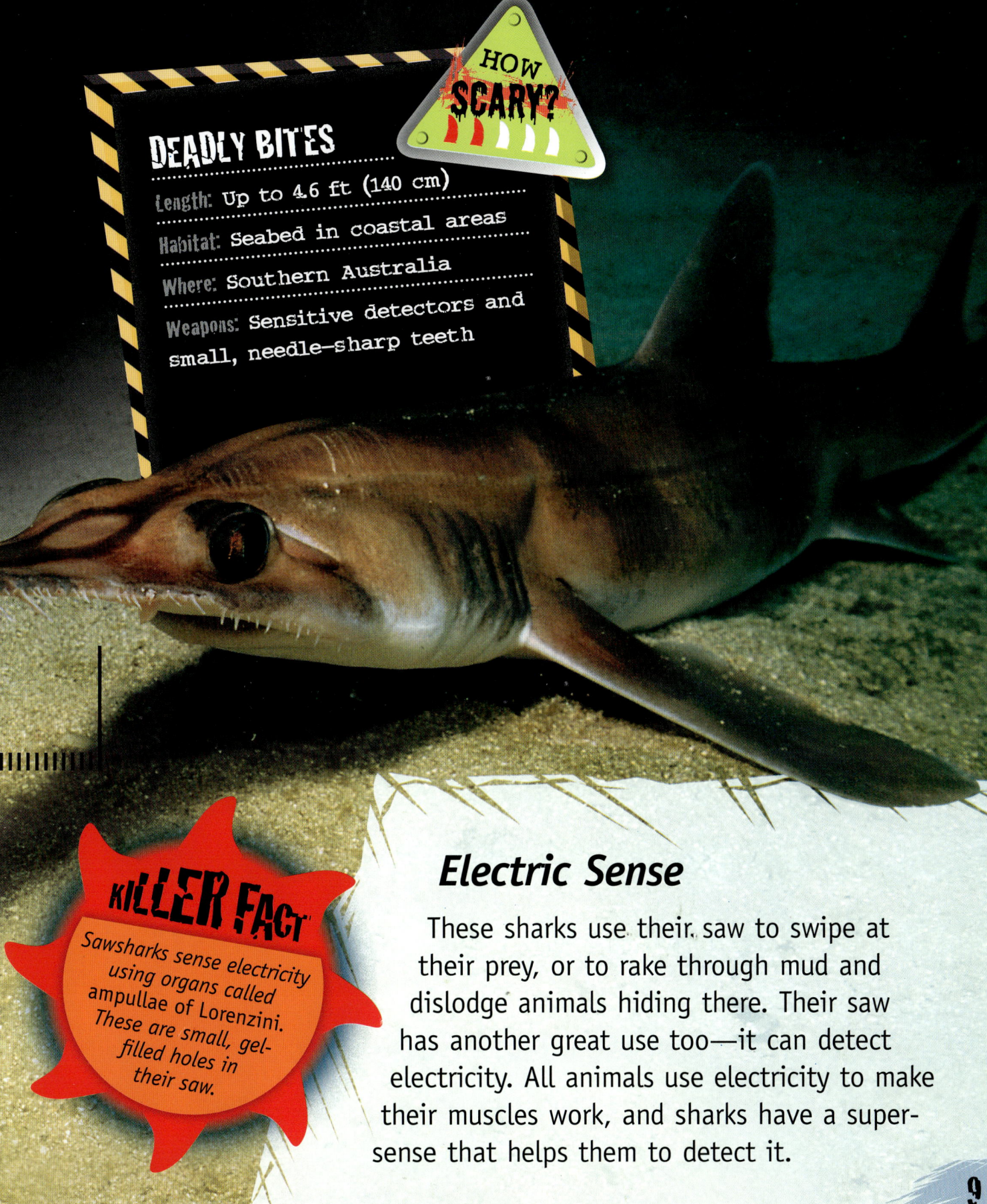

DEADLY BITES

Length: Up to 4.6 ft (140 cm)
Habitat: Seabed in coastal areas
Where: Southern Australia
Weapons: Sensitive detectors and small, needle-sharp teeth

HOW SCARY?

Killer Fact
Sawsharks sense electricity using organs called ampullae of Lorenzini. These are small, gel-filled holes in their saw.

Electric Sense

These sharks use their saw to swipe at their prey, or to rake through mud and dislodge animals hiding there. Their saw has another great use too—it can detect electricity. All animals use electricity to make their muscles work, and sharks have a super-sense that helps them to detect it.

SCUTIGERA

Creepy-crawlies, spiders, scorpions, and stinging bugs are some of the world's most incredible creatures. They belong to one enormous group of animals, called **invertebrates**.

DEADLY BITES

Length: 4 in. (10 cm)
Habitat: Dark, damp places
Where: Mostly in tropical regions
Weapons: Powerful, venom-injecting claws

HOW SCARY?

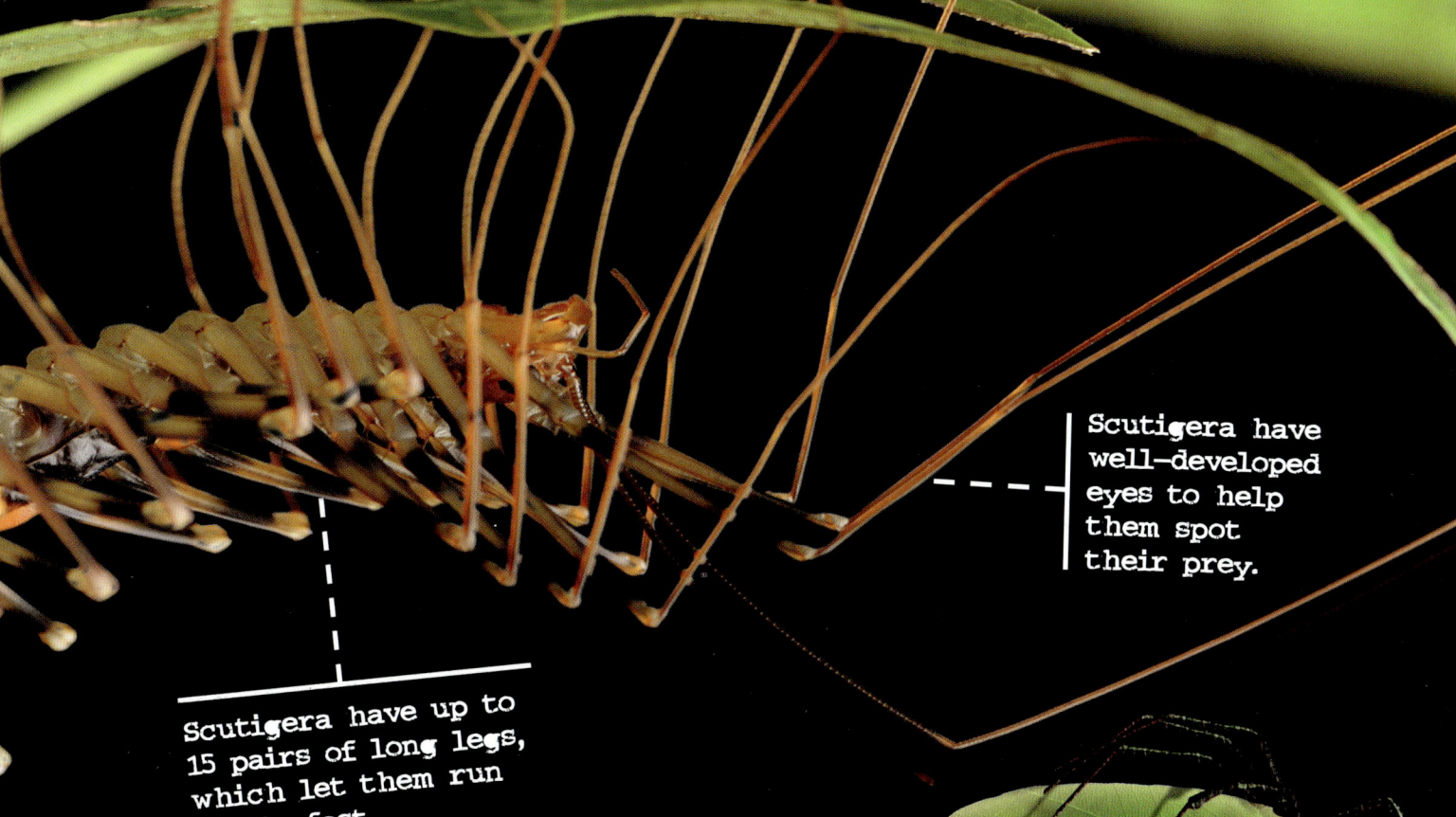

Scutigera have up to 15 pairs of long legs, which let them run really fast.

Scutigera have well-developed eyes to help them spot their prey.

KILLER FACT
The venom from some scutigera centipedes is strong enough to make a human very sick.

Invertebrates are usually small and they don't have bones, but many of them are still fearsome **predators**. This is a giant long-legged centipede called a scutigera. Its body is divided into parts called **segments**, and there is a pair of legs on most segments.

The first pair of legs has claws that can inject a deadly **venom** into a victim. Scutigera feed on other invertebrates, such as beetles.

Creepy Legs

Why does any bug need 15 pairs of legs? They aren't just for running—these limbs have another important job to do. This centipede uses its legs to feel its way in the dark, and to find prey.

GILA MONSTER

47 These lizards are called monsters for a good reason—they have venomous bites. Gila monsters mostly use their venom to defend themselves from other animals.

Gila monsters move slowly, so they pose very little risk to humans.

Gilas are slow-moving desert lizards that prey on birds' eggs and bugs. Like other reptiles, these lizards can use their tongues to sense if food is around. When they flick their tongues, they are "tasting" the air.

Big Digger

The Mexican beaded lizard also has a venomous bite. It uses its large claws to dig burrows, where it hides. It uses its venom to subdue prey, such as birds and small mammals. Its bite is believed to be harmless to humans.

KILLER FACT
Some people keep Gila monsters as pets, which is a bad idea. Eight people have died from Gila bites.

Many venomous animals prefer to warn their enemies away, rather than having to fight them. Gila monsters have black bodies with bold patterns of pink, yellow, or orange. These colors warn predators that the lizards are venomous.

DEADLY BITES
Length: 19.7 in. (50 cm)
Habitat: Deserts
Where: Southwestern United States and Mexico
Weapons: Sharp teeth and a venomous bite

HOW SCARY?

ALLIGATOR SNAPPING TURTLE

46 This reptilian predator lurks beneath the murky water in swamps. When it lifts its ugly, scaly head above the water, the bad-tempered animal snaps its jaws and does a great impression of a prehistoric monster. Alligator snapping turtles have one of the nastiest bites of any animal. They grow large and heavy, and live in **freshwater** where they feed on fish. Snapping turtles can reach the age of 100 or more.

With their spiked shells, these reptiles are known as the dinosaurs of the turtle world.

REPTILE BITES
Length: 31.5 in. (80 cm)
Habitat: Lakes, rivers, and swamps
Where: Southeastern USA
Weapons: Scissor-sharp jaws and a vicious bite

HOW SCARY?

Not What It Seems!

When a fish approaches a little red, wriggling worm, it has no idea it is swimming into the jaws of death. For that is no worm, but a lure—a wormlike lump of flesh inside the turtle's mouth that tempts fish and frogs to come close—SNAP!

Killer Fact

When the turtle sees food, it fills its lure with blood so that it looks red, plump, and very tasty!

SECRETARY BIRD

Raptors have curved bills, which they use to tear the flesh of their prey.

45 Birds of prey—raptors—are masters of the sky. Most of them have sharp **talons**, hooked bills, and huge wings that allow them to swoop through the skies looking for prey.

Killer Fact
Secretary birds flap their wings when they attack a snake to draw its attention away from the bird's face.

Secretary birds have long legs that allow them to run at high speed.

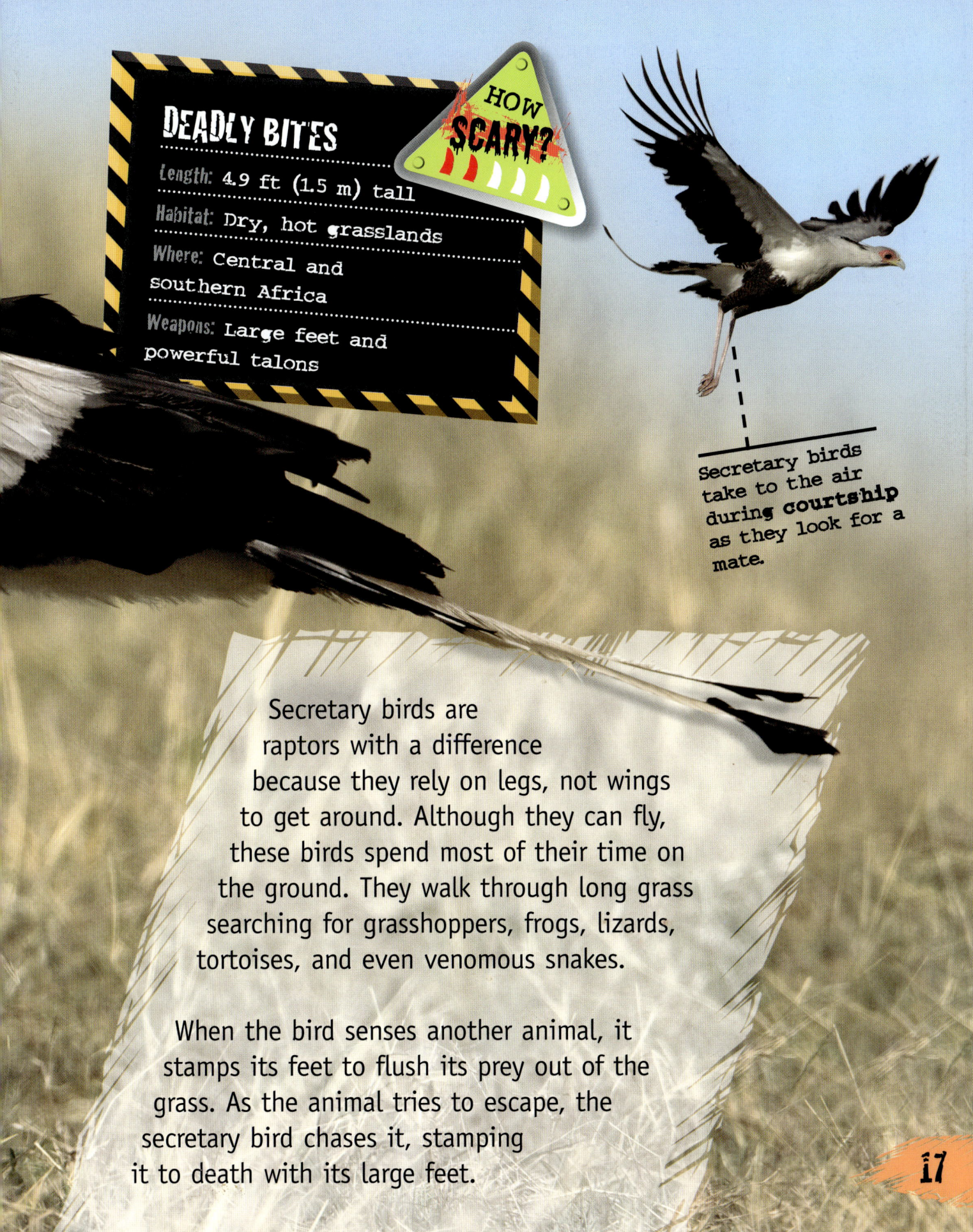

DEADLY BITES

Length: 4.9 ft (1.5 m) tall
Habitat: Dry, hot grasslands
Where: Central and southern Africa
Weapons: Large feet and powerful talons

HOW SCARY?

Secretary birds take to the air during **courtship** as they look for a mate.

Secretary birds are raptors with a difference because they rely on legs, not wings to get around. Although they can fly, these birds spend most of their time on the ground. They walk through long grass searching for grasshoppers, frogs, lizards, tortoises, and even venomous snakes.

When the bird senses another animal, it stamps its feet to flush its prey out of the grass. As the animal tries to escape, the secretary bird chases it, stamping it to death with its large feet.

VAMPIRE BAT

KILLER FACT
Vampire bats have special heat-sensing areas on their noses that help them to find their prey.

41 There are few predators with a worse reputation than the little vampire bat. That's no wonder given their ugly faces, nasty "**fangs**," and a feeding habit of drinking blood.

Vampire bats sense warm bodies with their noses.

DEADLY BITES

Length: 3.75 in. (95 mm) long

Habitat: Forests, grasslands, and deserts

Where: Central and South America

Weapons: Sharp little teeth

HOW SCARY?

Vampire bats can run at speeds of up to 5 miles (8 km) per hour.

7 in. (18 cm)

Actual size!

Bats' wings are made of long bones with skin stretched between them.

Bats are mammals. That means they have furry bodies and feed their young with milk. They are the only true flying mammals in the world. Most bats hunt flying prey, such as moths.

Vampire bats, however, feed on blood. They scuttle along the ground searching for warm bodies. A vampire bat bites through its victim's skin with its tiny teeth. As blood oozes out, the bat laps it up.

Pain-Free Feeding

A vampire bat's sharp teeth can tear through skin without the victim feeling pain. The bats produce a chemical that lessens the pain. Grooves in their tongues help blood to pour into their throats.

ELECTRIC EEL

43 Not all predators rely on jaws and claws to catch their prey. Electric eels are fish that **stun** and kill their prey in the most shocking way!

KILLER FACT
Electric eels may be fish, but they breathe air—like us. They often have to come to the river's surface to gulp air.

These fish live in the dark, murky waters of the Amazon River, where finding food is a challenge. Electric eels don't have good eyesight. Instead, they use weak electric pulses to find their way, like a **radar** system.

An electric eel also has electric organs along the length of its body. These are used to produce sudden electric shocks that stun the eel's prey or any predators that come too close.

The shock from an electric eel is strong enough to knock a horse off its feet.

DEADLY BITES

Length: 8.2 ft (250 cm)
Habitat: Rivers
Where: Northern areas in South America
Weapons: Electricity

HOW SCARY?

Sit and Wait

Moray eels lurk in dark places and wait for food to swim by. They have two sets of jaws to grab their prey and drag it down into their throats. Some morays also have **toxins** on their skins.

Moray eels have large teeth, which they use to tear the flesh of their prey.

ARMY ANT

KILLER FACT
One **colony** of army ants can kill up to 100,000 bugs in one day. Flies follow them around and eat any leftovers.

42 Few things can stop a horde of army ants when they go on a march. By working together, these insects are more powerful than many predators.

Huge jaws can cut and slice, breaking up victims' bodies into small pieces in minutes.

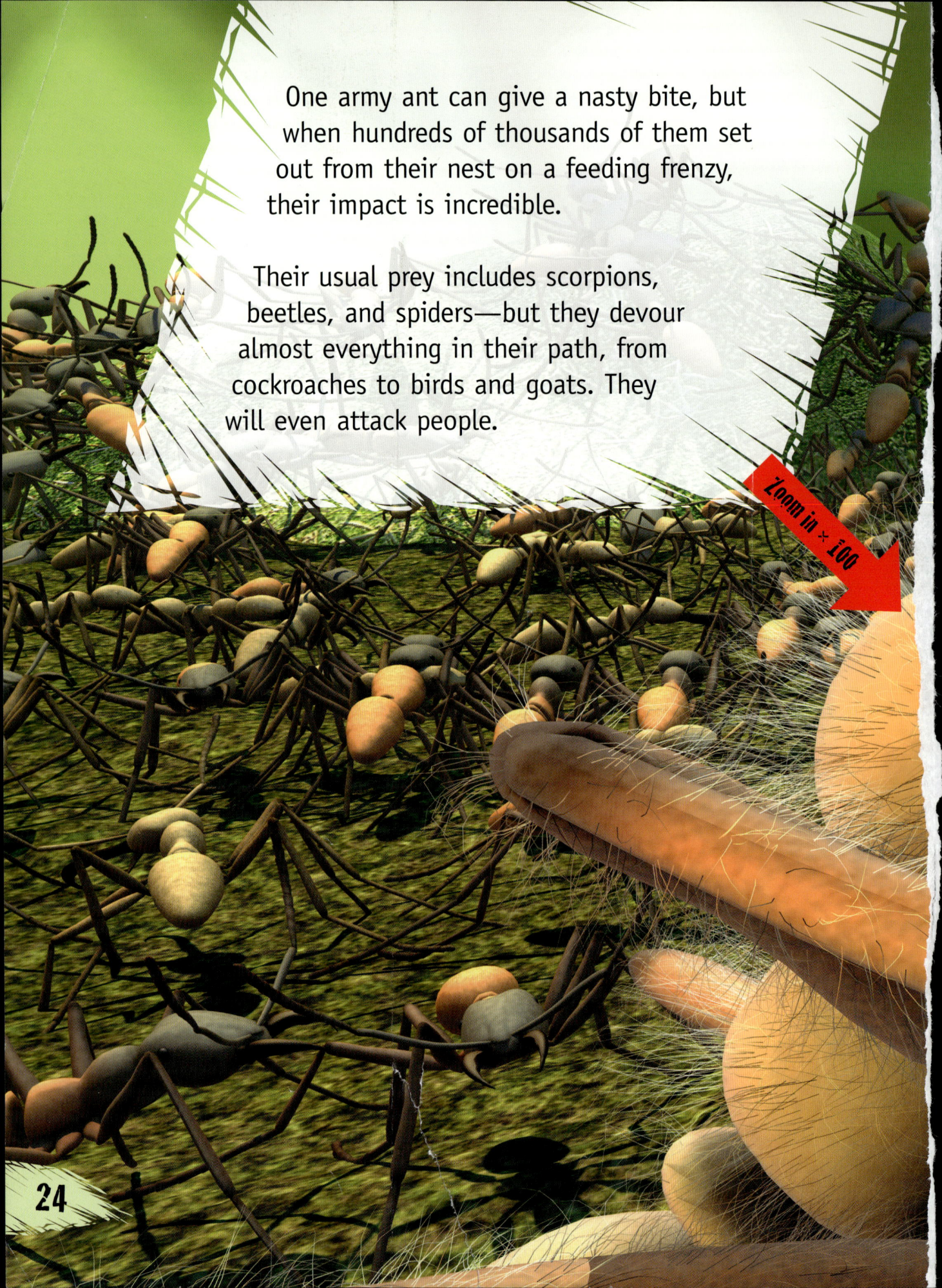

One army ant can give a nasty bite, but when hundreds of thousands of them set out from their nest on a feeding frenzy, their impact is incredible.

Their usual prey includes scorpions, beetles, and spiders—but they devour almost everything in their path, from cockroaches to birds and goats. They will even attack people.

Zoom in × 100

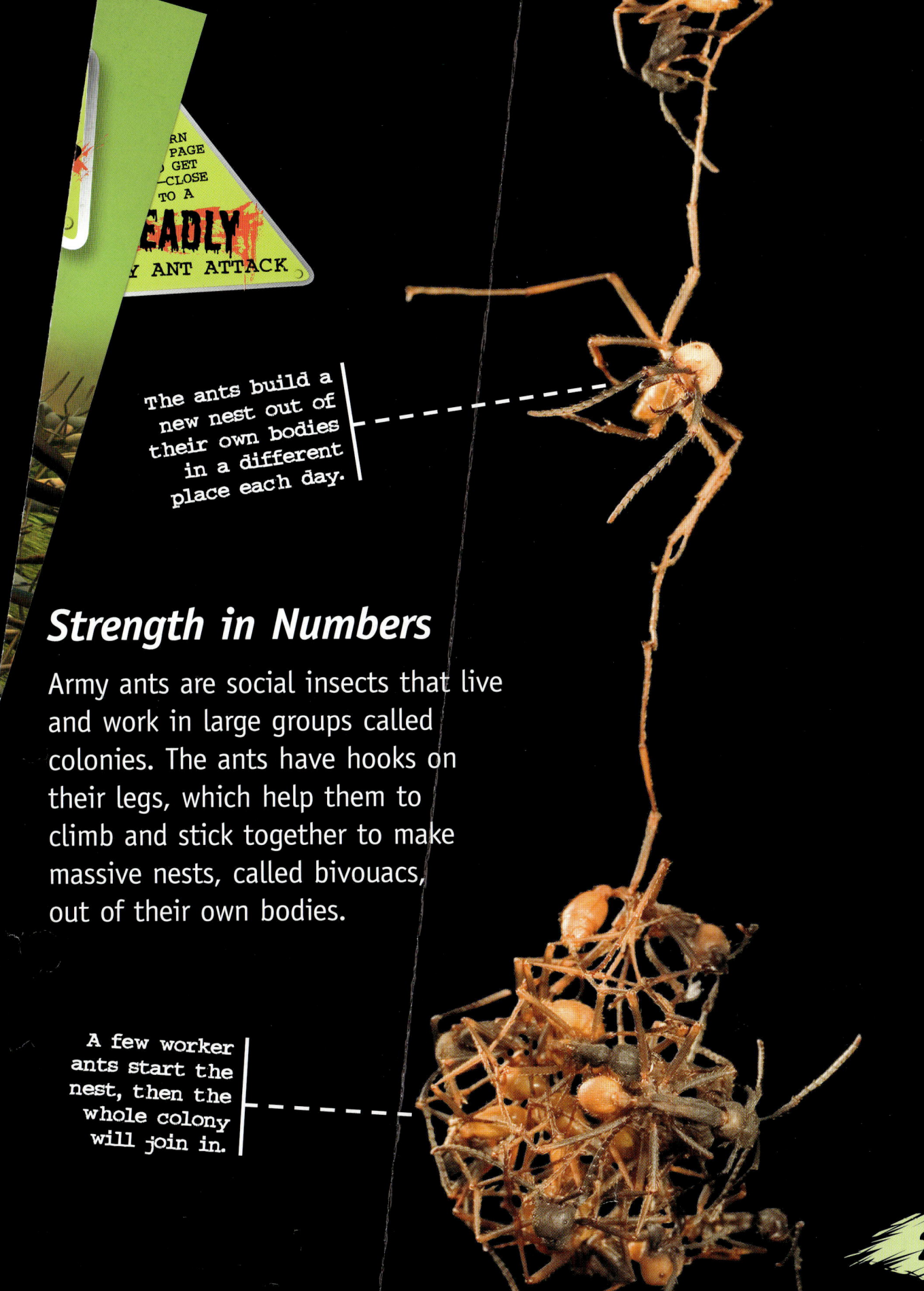

TURN THE PAGE TO GET UP-CLOSE TO A **DEADLY** ARMY ANT ATTACK

The ants build a new nest out of their own bodies in a different place each day.

Strength in Numbers

Army ants are social insects that live and work in large groups called colonies. The ants have hooks on their legs, which help them to climb and stick together to make massive nests, called bivouacs, out of their own bodies.

A few worker ants start the nest, then the whole colony will join in.

DEADLY BITES

Length: 0.6 in. (15 mm)
Habitat: Hot and humid forests
Where: Australia
Weapons: Powerful jaws, stingers, and lots of friends

HOW SCARY!

TASMANIAN DEVIL

KILLER FACT
Tasmanian devils have pink ears, which turn red when they are very angry!

41 Tasmanian devils deserve their name—they are ferocious and extremely bad-tempered. Devils are famous for their blood-curdling nighttime screeches!

Flexible front feet allow devils to hold their food.

Food Fight

Tasmanian devils have a great sense of smell. If one devil is feeding, others detect the smell and rush over to share in the feast. Fights sometimes break out over food, but usually the hungry animals just growl at one another.

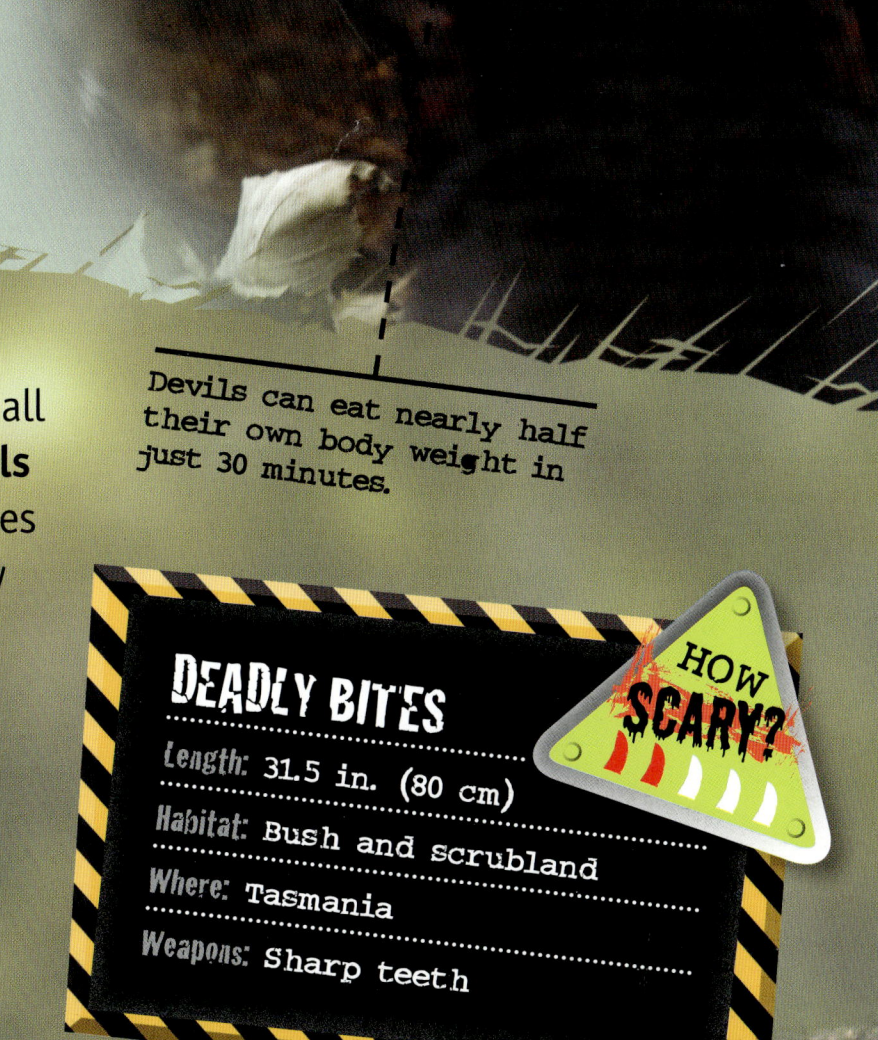

Devils can eat nearly half their own body weight in just 30 minutes.

Tasmanian devils look like small bears, but they are **marsupials**—a type of mammal that gives birth to tiny young that grow inside a pouch.

These predators survive on a diet of meat, which they get by killing animals, such as wallabies and possums, or by scavenging.

DEADLY BITES

Length: 31.5 in. (80 cm)
Habitat: Bush and scrubland
Where: Tasmania
Weapons: Sharp teeth

HOW SCARY?

SEA SNAKE

Sea snakes are venomous snakes that have taken to living and hunting underwater. Some sea snakes give birth to live baby snakes in water, while others come onto land to lay their eggs. They all have to come to the surface to breathe.

KILLER FACT
Sea snakes are known for their mild tempers, and it is very difficult to make one angry enough to bite.

DEADLY BITES
Length: 43 in. (110 cm)
Habitat: Shallow ocean water
Where: Pacific and Indian Oceans, Arabian Gulf
Weapons: Fangs with a muscle-eating venom

HOW SCARY?

Sea snakes have more powerful venom than any other snakes, but they rarely bite people and have small fangs. Sea snakes feed on small fish and mollusks.

If they do bite, sea snakes inject only a tiny amount of venom and their victims may not even know they have been bitten at first. The venom causes muscles to break down, and death can occur in a few hours.

Sea snakes swim slowly along the ocean floor looking for prey.

Land and Sea

Sea snakes called kraits come ashore to **shed** their old skins, to mate, and to lay their eggs. The females lay three to 10 eggs in old burrows left by seabirds or under rocks.

Like all snakes, kraits live alone, only coming together to mate.

PIRANHA

39 It is said that a group of piranhas can strip the body of a cow to the bones in minutes. The truth is nowhere near as frightening! These fish can live in large groups called shoals, but they mostly feed on bugs, small fish, and shrimps.

Piranha teeth are pointed and razor-sharp.

Actual size!

DEADLY BITES

Length: 13 in. (33 cm) long

Habitat: Rivers

Where: South America

Weapons: Sharp teeth

HOW SCARY?

Slice and Slash

Piranhas are able to devour flesh easily, because their strong jaws are lined with large, triangular teeth that interlock perfectly to make a cutting machine that can slash and slice.

Killer Fact

People who have been bitten by piranhas have had entire fingers or toes cleanly sliced off!

Piranhas feed at dawn and dusk, when there is little sunlight and they can hide behind water plants, often in groups of up to 30 fish. Most piranhas attack prey alone.

Occasionally, a number of shoals may gather together into a much larger group to attack and feast on a large animal. However, this is very rare and probably only happens when there is a shortage of food.

KILLER BEE

38 One bee on its own is unlikely to do much harm to a person. When a group of bees gets together, it's a different matter. A buzzing, angry swarm is terrifying—and dangerous.

Killer bees will chase an animal over longer distances than normal bees.

DEADLY BITES

Length: 0.75 in. (2 cm)

Habitat: Where flowers grow

Where: South and Central America, United States

Weapons: Venomous sting

HOW SCARY?

Fast Fighters

Killer bees are much more likely to attack than ordinary bees. They are quick to create huge angry swarms and can detect people 49 feet (15 m) away from their nests.

KILLER FACT

Bees die after one sting. Wasps and hornets can keep stinging until they run out of venom.

Bees feed on nectar and pollen from flowers, so they will only sting other animals or people to defend themselves from attack. Most bees have a single sting with tiny hooks called barbs on it. The barbs help the sting to stay in the victim, while venom is pumped into the victim's body, causing pain and swelling.

The sting of a killer bee is no worse than any other bee. It is only a problem when an animal is stung lots of times.

DEADLY SHARKS

A giant fish swims through the ocean, and its body casts a dark shadow on the seabed below. With its huge teeth, super speed, and cold, dead eyes, this shark is one of the world's most impressive predators.

Most sharks are long and thin, but they come in all shapes and sizes. The largest fish in the world is the mighty whale shark. It is harmless to people because it feeds on tiny animals called plankton.

Whale sharks are the giants of the ocean and grow to about 36 feet (11 meters) in length.

Frilled sharks have long, thin bodies and live deep underwater.

KILLER FACT

Sharks have been around for 400 million years, and had few predators—until humans began to hunt them.

All sharks are fish. They eat other animals, such as fish and squid. Sometimes, sharks mistake humans for food and attack them. Most sharks are wary of humans, and try to avoid them. There are some scary ones, however, that are more aggressive.

This blue shark has a pointed nose, or snout, and large eyes so that it can see well in deep water.

LEMON SHARK

37 Lemon sharks are large coastal sharks. They prefer to live in warm, shallow waters near land, especially during the day. At night they swim to deeper water.

Lemon sharks have a wide, flat head.

DEADLY BITES

Length: Up to 11 ft (340 cm)

Habitat: Reefs, mangroves, bays, and river mouths

Where: Warm American waters and West Africa

Weapons: Special electrical sensors and triangular teeth

HOW SCARY?

Lemon sharks have small eyes and poor eyesight. The coastal waters where they live are often cloudy, so eyesight is not a great help in finding prey. Instead, these fish have special magnetic **sensors** in their snout, which help them to find fish and shelled animals on the seabed.

Sharksuckers

Remoras, or sharksuckers, are long, thin fish with a special ability. They have a sucker on the top of their head, which they use to stick to a shark or other large fish and hitch a ride. They feed off any scraps that the shark does not eat.

Lemon sharks get their name from the yellow-brown color of their skin.

EGGS AND PUPS

Most fish lay eggs that **hatch** into baby fish. Sharks are special, though. Many of them don't lay eggs, they give birth to their young instead. Young sharks are called **pups**.

Lemon sharks can give birth to as many as 17 pups in a single year.

Most mother sharks keep their pups inside their body while they grow. This means the pups are protected from predators for as long as possible. When the pups are born they are able to swim away. Sharks don't look after their pups.

Mermaid's Purse

Sharks that do lay eggs, such as catsharks, lay the eggs in a thick, rubbery case called a mermaid's purse. These egg cases often have curly strings, which attach them to rocks or seaweed to stop them from floating away. The shark pups grow inside for up to ten months.

Up to 3.2 in (8 cm)

Actual size!

This newborn lemon shark pup swims away from its mother.

Killer Fact

Pups growing inside their mother may eat each other before they are even born. Sometimes only one or two pups survive.

JUMPER ANT

36 There are at least 10,000 **species** of ant in the world. Most ants can bite or sting—or make venomous droplets that inflict pain. Their venom is similar to that of bees.

KILLER FACT

Many people are allergic to the chemicals in these ants' stings, and can become seriously sick after one bite.

This jumper ant has managed to catch a bee in its jaws.

Bulldog and jumper ants are larger than most ants, and use their excellent eyesight to find other ants and bees to prey on. They are aggressive insects that will leap into action when they are threatened—and can actually jump at a victim!

Big Stingers

Little black bullet ants are said to inflict the most painful of all ant stings. Fire ants use their stings to defend the large homes they make and share. They use their pincers to grab hold of their victim and just keep on stinging!

As jumper ants sink their large jaws into an animal or human, they use a stinger to inject powerful chemicals that cause great pain.

DEADLY BITES

Length: 1 in. (25 mm)
Habitat: Forests
Where: Australia
Weapons: Strong jaws and a painful stinger

HOW SCARY?

LONOMIA

KILLER FACT
Scientists hope to be able to make life-saving medicine using lonomia venom.

35 A killer caterpillar's deadly spines send out a clear warning to predators—this creature will not make a tasty snack.

The colorful caterpillar becomes a brown moth.

A lonomia caterpillar will become a moth one day. While it is still young, however, a caterpillar's job is to eat and grow—and avoid being eaten itself.

Most caterpillars rely on **camouflage** to stay safe. They are often green or brown so they can hide on the plants they eat. Lonomia caterpillars, however, are covered with sharp spines that they want predators to notice!

Prickles and Poison

The sharp spines warn predators, such as birds, lizards, and frogs, that this soft-bodied mini monster is carrying a nasty venom. The spines break when they pierce a victim's skin, and the venom enters its body.

The bright colors help to warn predators.

If enough venom gets into a person's body, it can cause severe pain, bruising, and even death!

DEADLY BITES

Length: 2.4 in. (6 cm) long
Habitat: Rain forests
Where: South America
Weapons: Venom-tipped spines all over its body

HOW SCARY?

43

PARALYSIS TICK

KILLER FACT
Other ticks also cause disease. They carry bacteria that infect the wounds they make.

34 Ticks are insects with eight legs, like spiders, and a blood-sucking lifestyle. Most ticks cause little harm, but some of them carry a deadly secret.

These bugs are **parasites**, which means they feed on another animal while it is still alive. Ticks have sharp mouthparts that pierce a hole in a victim's flesh, and inject a liquid to stop blood from **clotting**. The ticks suck blood until their bodies are large and swollen, and then they fall to the ground.

Actual sizes!
Before feeding
After feeding

Australian paralysis ticks have another nasty trick. They don't just suck blood—they inject a venom that causes the victim to become **paralyzed**. Without treatment, the victim may die.

44

Paralysis ticks prey on many kinds of animal, including pets and people.

DEADLY BITES

Length: 0.16 in. (4 mm)
Habitat: Hot and humid forests
Where: Australia
Weapons: A big appetite and some harmful diseases

HOW SCARY?

Tick **larvae** have three pairs of legs, while adult ticks have four pairs.

Only a small number of tick **eggs** will actually hatch.

Monster Moms

Female ticks must feed on blood before they can lay eggs, and this is when they inject dangerous toxins. They lay up to 3,000 eggs at a time. Lazy males sometimes suck blood from the females!

45

GRAY REEF SHARK

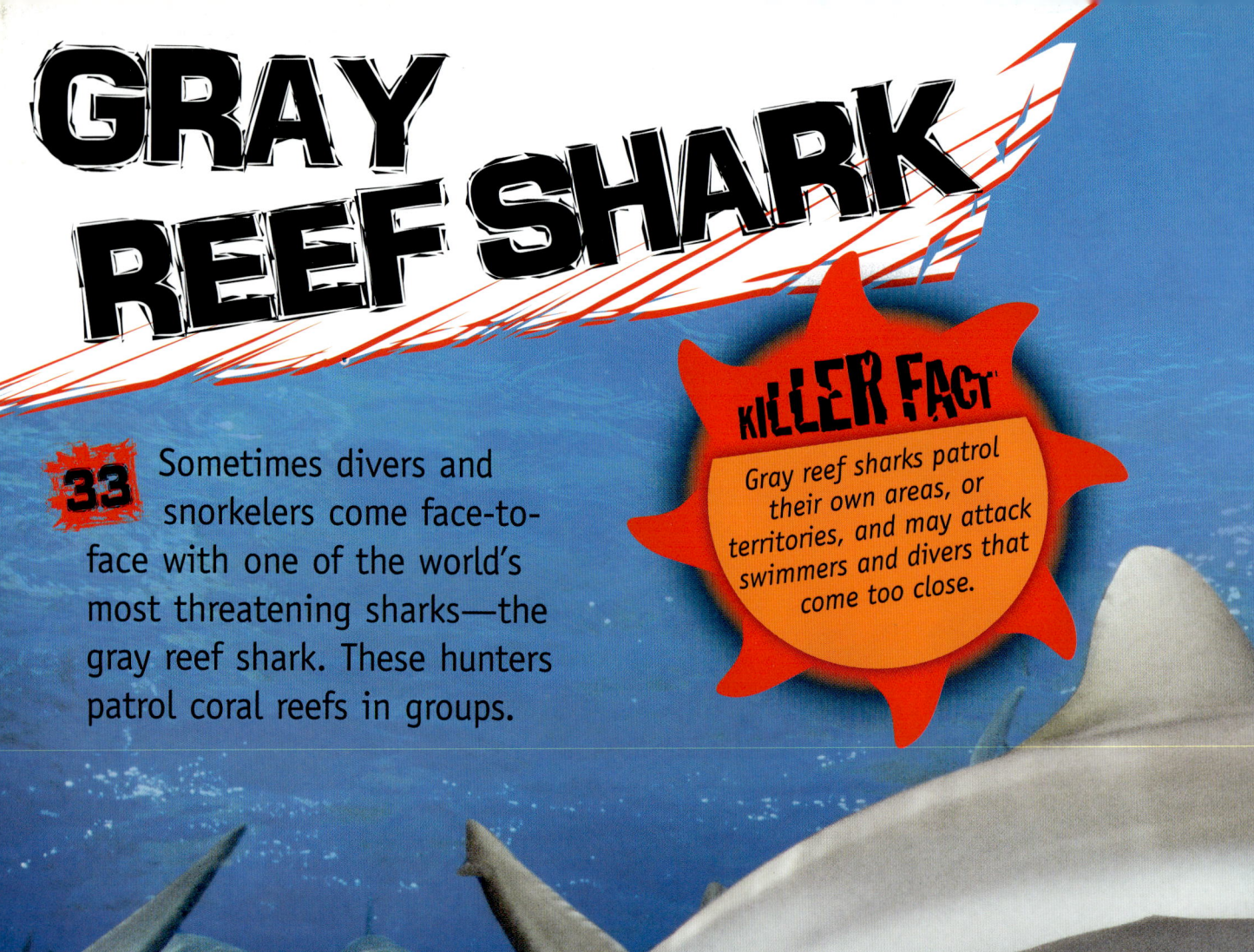

33 Sometimes divers and snorkelers come face-to-face with one of the world's most threatening sharks—the gray reef shark. These hunters patrol coral reefs in groups.

KILLER FACT
Gray reef sharks patrol their own areas, or territories, and may attack swimmers and divers that come too close.

Most sharks are **solitary** animals and live alone. Gray reef sharks, however, often swim in groups in quiet spots during the day. At night they go their separate ways to hunt. When a gray reef shark is feeling threatened it raises its snout, arches its back, and swims with a swaying motion. This menacing behavior warns enemies to move away—or prepare to be attacked.

Fishy Feasts

Gray reef sharks feed on squid, octopus, and small shelled animals such as shrimp and lobsters. They also prey on the colorful fish that live among the reefs, such as these beautiful butterfly fish.

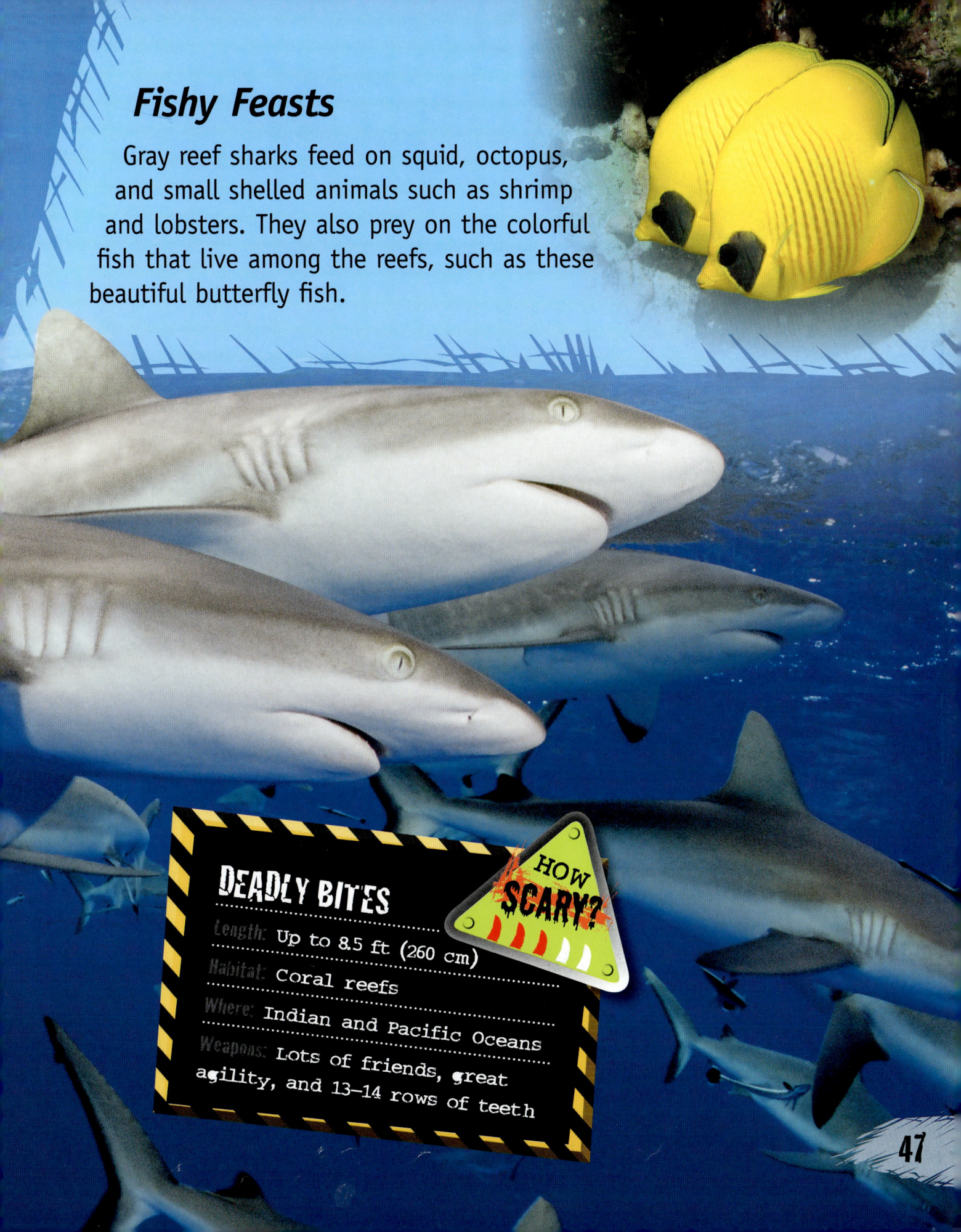

DEADLY BITES

Length: Up to 8.5 ft (260 cm)
Habitat: Coral reefs
Where: Indian and Pacific Oceans
Weapons: Lots of friends, great agility, and 13–14 rows of teeth

HOW SCARY?

CHIMPANZEE

32 Some animal experts think chimpanzees are among the most impressive of all predators. They are fast and clever, and work in a gang to track and kill other animals.

When they feel threatened, chimps bare their teeth.

Toolmakers

Like humans, chimps make tools to use in a hunt. They strip bark from a branch, sharpen it, and use it to kill small animals. They also use twigs to dig into termite nests.

KILLER FACT
Chimpanzees are our closest living relatives and some of the cleverest animals alive.

For a long time, scientists thought chimps enjoyed a diet of fruits, leaves, nuts, roots, and bugs. Then it was discovered they also prey on pigs and monkeys, and even kill chimps from other families.

These apes hunt cooperatively, which means they work together and have different jobs to do. One chimp might chase a monkey through the trees, while another blocks its escape route and a third waits to **ambush** it.

DEADLY BITES
- Length: 35.4 in. (90 cm) tall
- Habitat: Tropical rain forest
- Where: Central Africa
- Weapons: Hands and teeth

HOW SCARY?

HONEY BADGER

31 Honey badgers may have a sweet-sounding name, but they are totally fearless predators. These beasts are programmed to strike and kill, and they are not fussy about what they attack.

KILLER FACT
Honey badgers can kill small crocodiles and pythons that are more than 10 feet (3 m) long!

Badgers live alone and only come together once a year to breed.

These predators explore every avenue in pursuit of food. They dig holes in the ground, searching for worms and bugs, climb trees to raid honey and grubs from bees' nests, and even scamper to upper branches to steal eggs from raptor nests!

DEADLY BITES

Length: 30.3 in. (77 cm) long
Habitat: Forests and mountains
Where: Parts of Africa and Asia
Weapons: Sharp teeth and claws

HOW SCARY?

It takes courage to face a lion devouring its prey head on, and then scare that lion away. But that's what honey badgers are willing to do when they have their sights set on lunch.

Thick skin around the neck and small ears protect the honey badger from injury in fights.

Best Friends

Honeyguide birds perch near to bees' nests, and show honey badgers where to dig or climb. Once the badger has opened a nest, the bird swoops in to feast on bees and beeswax.

KOMODO DRAGON

KILLER FACT
Komodo Island has become a huge wildlife park where the dragons are protected.

DEADLY BITES
- **Length:** 9.8 ft. (3 m)
- **Habitat:** Scrubland and grassland
- **Where:** Komodo Island, Indonesia
- **Weapons:** Big claws and a venomous bite

HOW SCARY?

30 Few predators are more fascinating than the Komodo dragon. These huge reptiles rule the island of Komodo in Indonesia, but there are fewer than 5,000 of them left in the wild.

Komodos were not discovered until about 100 years ago.

Komodos are the world's heaviest lizards, and a male can weigh more than an adult human. They have strength rather than speed, and lie in wait for passing prey to ambush it. Komodos aren't fussy and will eat almost anything they find, including deer, pigs— and even humans!

Deadly Bite

When a Komodo spots its prey, it springs to action and uses its sharp claws to hold the animal down. A quick bite with its sharp teeth allows the Komodo to pass venom into the prey's body. The injured animal runs away, but will soon weaken from its wound. The Komodo can then stroll over and finish its meal.

One side of a Komodo's teeth has jagged **serrations**.

KING COBRA

A king cobra puffs out its hood when threatened to make itself look bigger.

29 The king cobra is the longest of all venomous snakes, and can reach a length of more than 16 feet (5 m). It's so big, a king cobra can raise enough of its body off the ground to look a human in the eye!

As hunters, king cobras have powerful venom and size on their side, but they prey on other snakes, not people. When they are scared, these snakes rear up, spread out their hoods, and hiss. Putting on this scary show is a type of defense and it should make most enemies think twice before coming any closer.

DEADLY BITES
Length: 16 ft. (5 m)
Habitat: Forests, grassland, and scrubland
Where: Southeast Asia
Weapons: Fangs with deadly venom

HOW SCARY?

Killer Fact
King cobras rarely kill people, but Indian cobras attack at least 10,000 people every year in India alone.

Mamba!

28 Everyone in Africa knows to look out for this snake, which is one of the world's most dangerous predators. Mambas can slither faster than a person can run, are active during daytime, and have a deadly bite. Thankfully, mambas normally hunt birds and small animals—not people.

One bite from a mamba can kill an adult human in minutes.

Actual size!

HAMMERHEAD SHARK

27 There are about 400 different types, or species, of shark and some of the strangest-looking ones are called hammerheads. Like its relatives—such as the mallethead sharks—the great hammerhead has an extraordinary appearance.

A hammerhead's nostrils are far apart, helping it to sense the direction of different smells.

A hammerhead's head is huge and wide, with eyes positioned right at the very ends. This shape probably helps the predator to move through water and change direction. The position of its eyes helps the shark to focus on its prey more easily, and work out how far away it is.

KILLER FACT

Hammerheads like to feast on venomous stingrays, and can even eat the venom-filled tails!

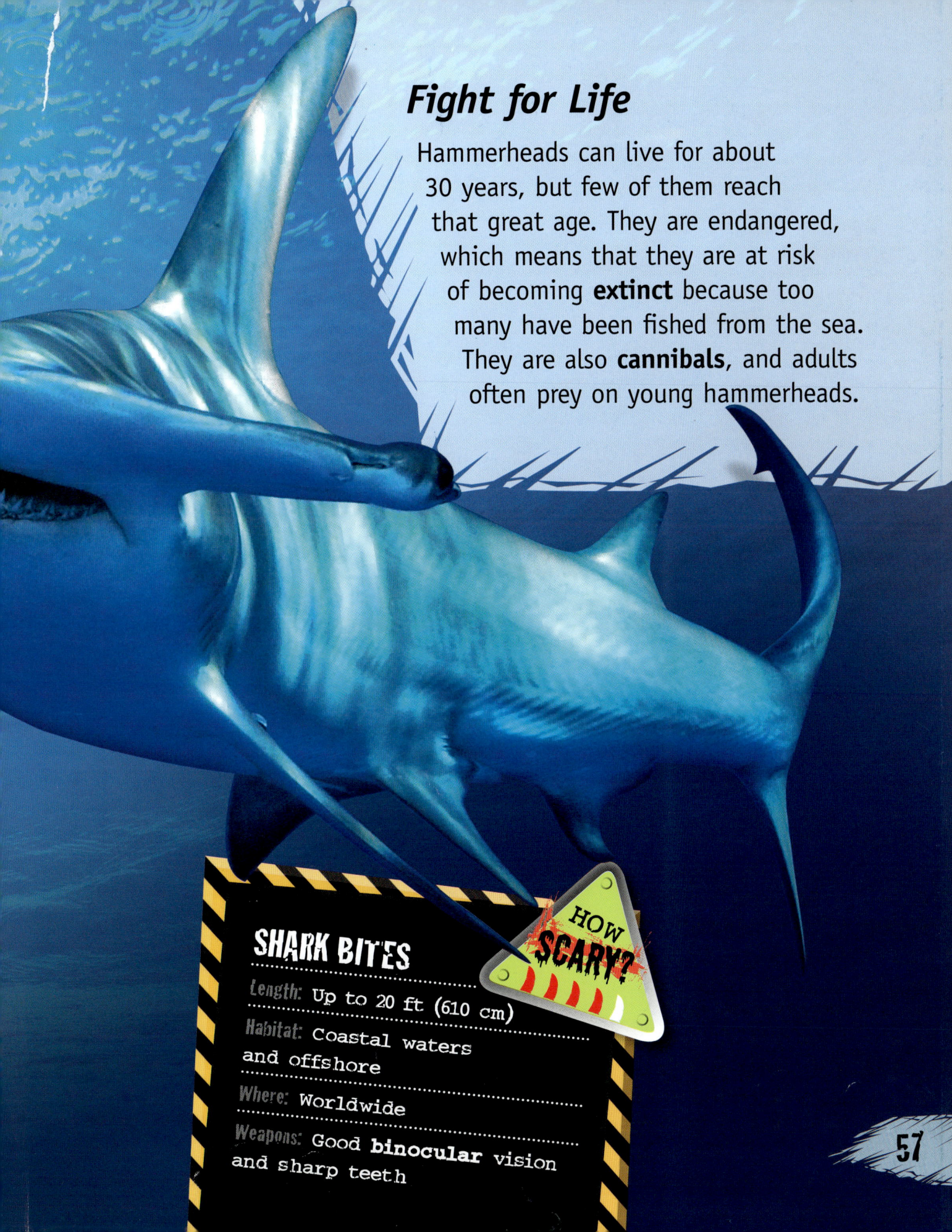

Fight for Life

Hammerheads can live for about 30 years, but few of them reach that great age. They are endangered, which means that they are at risk of becoming **extinct** because too many have been fished from the sea. They are also **cannibals**, and adults often prey on young hammerheads.

SHARK BITES

Length: Up to 20 ft (610 cm)
Habitat: Coastal waters and offshore
Where: Worldwide
Weapons: Good **binocular** vision and sharp teeth

HOW SCARY?

CORAL SNAKE

26 Look at the two snakes shown on these pages. Can you tell the difference? The coral snake in the main picture has red and yellow bands that warn predators of its venomous bite, but the milk snake opposite is a harmless copycat.

Coral snakes hunt lizards, snakes, frogs, nesting birds, and small mammals.

The yellow bands on this snake's body are next to the red color. This means it is a deadly coral snake.

REPTILE BITES

HOW SCARY?

Length: 35 in. (90 cm)

Habitat: Forests

Where: The Americas

Weapons: Fangs with deadly venom

KILLER FACT
Coral snake venom stops nerves and muscles working. **Antivenoms** often save lives.

There are about 40 different types of coral snake, with different patterns of colored bands. Most live in burrows and only come out at night, so humans rarely encounter these venomous creatures.

Coral snakes need to keep jabbing at a victim to inject all their venom, so although the venom is deadly in large amounts, it is rare for people to die following an attack.

Smart Mimic

Milk snakes can bite, but they don't have venom. Their cunning disguise, however, makes them look like venomous coral snakes so predators stay away. A rhyme helps identify some of these colorful snakes: *If red touches yellow, it can kill a fellow, if red touches black, it's a friend of Jack.*

TIGER

25 Tigers are the largest of all the big cats, and one of the largest of all predators. These majestic animals combine beauty, **stealth**, and speed with a deadly instinct to kill.

Most tigers live and hunt alone. They patrol their areas, which are called territories, looking for clues that other tigers or other animals are nearby. Tigers have a great sense of smell, which helps them to find prey hiding in the jungle.

A tiger's stripes camouflage it, keeping it hidden from its prey.

DEADLY BITES

HOW SCARY?

Length: Up to 9.1 ft. (280 cm)

Habitat: Forests, mountains, and jungles

Where: Southeast Asia

Weapons: Teeth and claws

KILLER FACT
There used to be eight species of tiger, but three of them have become extinct in the last 60 years.

The Siberian tiger lives high in the mountains, where it hunts deer and small mammals.

Big Appetites

Tigers can attack large animals, such as pigs, deer, and monkeys. They may even hunt baby elephants and rhinoceroses. Once it has killed its prey, a tiger will **gorge** itself on meat, eating up to 88 pounds (40 kg) at one time. It may keep returning to the carcass to feed on it over the next few days.

TURN THE PAGE TO GET UP-CLOSE TO A **DEADLY** TIGER

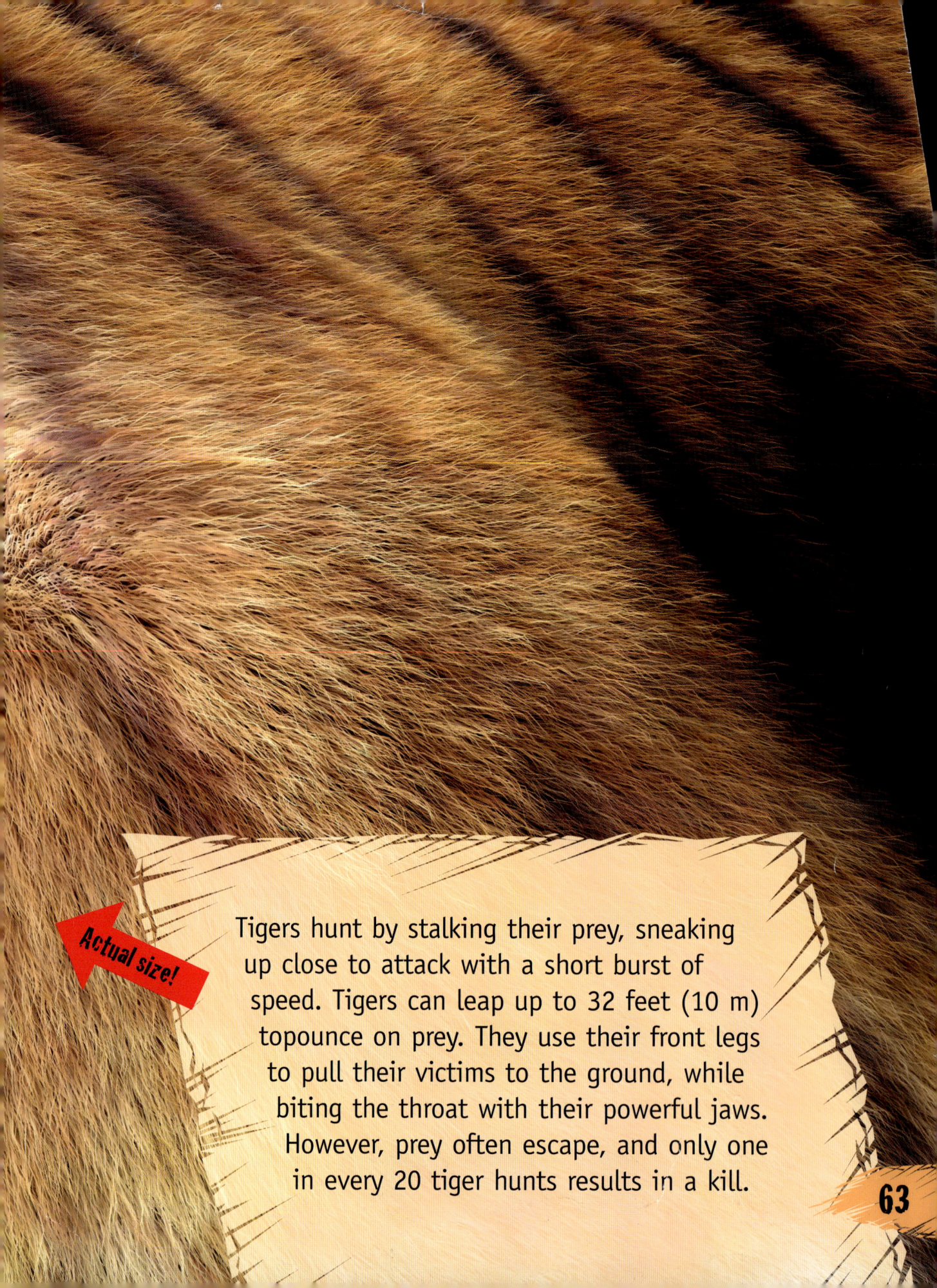

Actual size!

Tigers hunt by stalking their prey, sneaking up close to attack with a short burst of speed. Tigers can leap up to 32 feet (10 m) topounce on prey. They use their front legs to pull their victims to the ground, while biting the throat with their powerful jaws. However, prey often escape, and only one in every 20 tiger hunts results in a kill.

ANACONDA

24 Some fearsome reptiles take life at a slow pace, only stirring into action when hunger strikes. The **constrictor** snakes may survive for several months on one big meal!

Pythons and boas don't use deadly venom to kill their prey—they squeeze them to death instead. Anacondas are a type of boa. They spend most of their lives in water, but slither onto land to hunt. They ambush animals that come to the water to drink, grabbing them in their coils.

Anacondas wrap themselves around their prey and squeeze until it **suffocates**.

Killer Fact: Anacondas don't lay eggs. They give birth to up to 80 young snakes at a time.

A large anaconda is heavier than an adult human.

Massive Monsters

Anacondas are big enough to prey on large animals, including caimans, deer, and even people. A record-breaking anaconda measured 27.7 feet (8.4 m) long—as long as the net on a tennis court—and 43 inches (110 cm) around its middle.

Reptile Bites

Length: 28 ft. (8.5 m)

Habitat: Rain forests, grasslands, and rivers

Where: South America

Weapons: Constricting coils

How Scary?

BLACK CAIMAN

When caiman are underwater, special flaps close over their nostrils and ears to stop water from getting in.

23 Caimans are members of the crocodile and alligator family. Although they are great predators themselves, some types of caiman are close to extinction because humans hunt them for their skins.

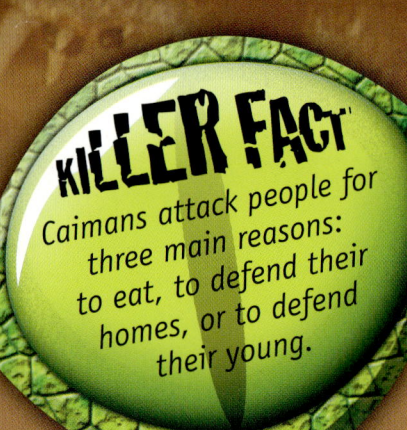

Killer Fact
Caimans attack people for three main reasons: to eat, to defend their homes, or to defend their young.

Caimans use their excellent eyesight and sense of smell to hunt fish, waterbirds, and turtles. They spend most of the day floating in water, but when they come ashore at night, they may hunt mammals, especially **capybaras**, dogs, pigs, and deer. They have been known to attack people.

REPTILE BITES

Length: 19.7 ft. (6 m)
Habitat: Rivers and lakes
Where: South America
Weapons: Sharp teeth

HOW SCARY?

The black caiman is the largest predator in the Amazon rain forest

Head is 2–3 in. (6–8 cm) long

Actual size!

Caring Mother

Female black caimans lay up to 60 eggs in a nest near slow-flowing water. They stay on their nest to protect their eggs from predators, and take care of the babies after they hatch.

67

BIRD-EATING SPIDER

22 This is no mini monster—it's a maxi monster! The goliath bird-eating spider is the heaviest spider in the world, and it attacks birds, lizards, and frogs.

All spiders have eight legs and a body that is divided into two parts. They can sense other animals through their legs, which are very sensitive to movement.

Goliath bird-eating spiders make a hissing noise to warn predators away. If that doesn't work, they rear up on their back legs and expose their fangs, ready to bite. They can also shoot irritating hairs at attackers.

Spiders use the hairs on their legs to sense the movements of other animals that are nearby.

10.25 in. (26 cm)

Actual size!

BUG BITES

Length: 10.25 in. (26 cm) across
Habitat: Mountain rain forests
Where: South America
Weapons: Enormous fangs, venom, and irritating hairs

HOW SCARY?

A Nasty Bite

The body of a goliath bird-eating spider can measure more than 4 inches (10 cm) and each fang is about 0.75 inches (2 cm) long. These spiders can inject venom when they bite.

KILLER FACT

Females can live for 20 years. Males rarely live for more than six years because they die after *mating*.

ASSASSIN BUG

21 Assassin bugs may be small, but they are deadly predators. These blood-sucking beasts hunt prey using a variety of cunning tricks.

KILLER FACT

Chagas disease, spread by assassin bugs, kills about 50,000 people a year, and causes heart disease in many survivors.

Assassin bugs hold on to prey using sticky pads on their front legs. Needle-like mouthparts pierce the victim's body and inject a toxic liquid that turns flesh into a tasty juice. A big cockroach takes just three seconds to die—and the bug then sucks up its liquid meal.

Some assassin bugs ambush their prey, or trick them by dangling dead insects near the entrance to their homes. Others pretend to be flies caught in a web, so they can pounce on the spider that comes to investigate.

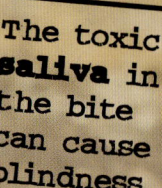

The toxic **saliva** in the bite can cause blindness.

This assassin bug is attacking a termite worker.

An assassin bug's bite is one of the most painful insect bites in the world.

Kissing Bug

Kissing bugs are assassin bugs that prey on larger animals, such as mammals, birds, and people. They suck blood from their victims and pass on the deadly Chagas disease.

BUG BITES

Length: 1.6 in. (4 cm)

Habitat: Many, from yards to forests

Where: Worldwide

Weapons: Needle-sharp bite that can inject bacteria

WOLVERINE

20 These weasellike animals are no bigger than a dog, but they are brave and fierce enough to attack a bear.

Wolverines live in the world's cold north, where food is scarce. They have long, thick fur to keep them warm.

These fearless predators are always on the move, and chase animals much bigger than themselves, such as deer. They leap boldly at their prey, grabbing them in their strong jaws.

Wolverines can kill prey that are many times bigger than them.

A wolverine's jaws are as powerful as those of a crocodile. They can crunch through the large bones of caribou and deer.

KILLER FACT
Wolverines are not just predators. They also scavenge, which means they eat dead animals they find.

Broad, furry paws help wolverines walk on icy surfaces.

PREDATOR BITES
Length: 39.4 in. (100 cm)
Habitat: Forests and mountains
Where: Northerly regions
Weapons: Massive jaws and crunching teeth

HOW SCARY?

WOLF

19 Wolves often appear in fairy tales and legends as wily killers. They are certainly smart predators with a nose for danger.

During the winter, wolves grow thick, fluffy fur.

PREDATOR BITES

Length: 4.9 ft. (150 cm)

Habitat: Cool forests and mountains

Where: Northerly places

Weapons: Sharp teeth and powerful jaws

HOW SCARY?

The alpha female is the only female in the pack that gives birth to cubs.

Rare Beasts

Wolves once roamed large parts of the world, but they are now mostly found in northern forests. They live in groups called packs that are ruled by a top male and female called the **alpha pair**.

When prey is nearby, wolves give chase and can run for hours. They work as a team, and may split up to confuse their prey and attack from all sides.

Powerful jaws can crush bones.

KILLER FACT
Gray wolves are the largest members of the dog family, and all of our pet dogs are descended from wolves.

Wolves keep in contact with each other over long distances by howling.

Like all dogs, wolves have an incredible sense of smell, and can detect prey, such as rabbits, by their smell more than a mile away. They can also hear sounds that are 6 miles (10 km) away.

BLACK WIDOW SPIDER

18 Black widow spiders are known as dangerous, but it's insects that have most to fear from their venomous attacks. Black widows set traps and deliver lethal bites.

KILLER FACT
Occasionally, female black widows kill and eat males after mating with them.

The spiders add drops of glue to the threads of a web to make them more sticky.

Black widows build messy webs using special bristles on their legs. Once the victim is trapped in the web, a spider can inject it with venom that is up to 15 times stronger than that of a rattlesnake, but in much smaller amounts.

Smart Moves

Most male spiders have to impress the females before mating. A male Australian redback spends more than an hour dancing for a female, but if she doesn't like his dance, she might eat him!

Black widows only bite people to defend themselves and their bites are rarely fatal.

BUG BITES

Length: 0.6 in. (15 mm)
Habitat: Warm, dark places
Where: North America
Weapons: A nasty bite, a sticky web, and strong venom

HOW SCARY?

SKELETONS AND SCALES

Most fish are bony fish. They have a bony skeleton that gives their body shape, power, and strength. Sharks, however, don't have bones. Instead, their skeleton is made from a strong, bendy material called **cartilage**.

KILLER FACT

It isn't just shark teeth that can hurt—their skin can too. Its rough surface can tear the skin from a swimmer's leg.

Shark denticles

This swell shark has a spotted pattern to help it hide against the seabed.

Shark skin is covered with scales that are coated with enamel—the same tough material that makes our teeth hard. These scales are called **denticles**. Denticles help water to move smoothly over a shark, so it can swim fast.

Colors and Patterns

Some sharks have interesting patterns. Colors and patterns can help a shark to stay hidden from view. This is called camouflage. This wobbegong shark's strange shape and frilled mouth make a good disguise.

TIGER SHARK

17 Meet the terrifying tiger shark—one of the most dangerous sharks in the world. These predators have been compared to garbage cans because they will try to eat almost anything.

They are called tiger sharks because their skin is marked with dark stripes and spots.

Tiger sharks are hungry, fearless hunters that come close to the shore in search of food. They spend most of the day slowly cruising through the water, but can suddenly burst into speed when they spy something tasty. They hunt sea turtles, clams, stingrays, sea snakes, seals, birds, and squid.

KiLLER FACT

Tiger shark teeth are serrated, like a saw. As the sharks bite, they pull their head from side to side and saw the flesh.

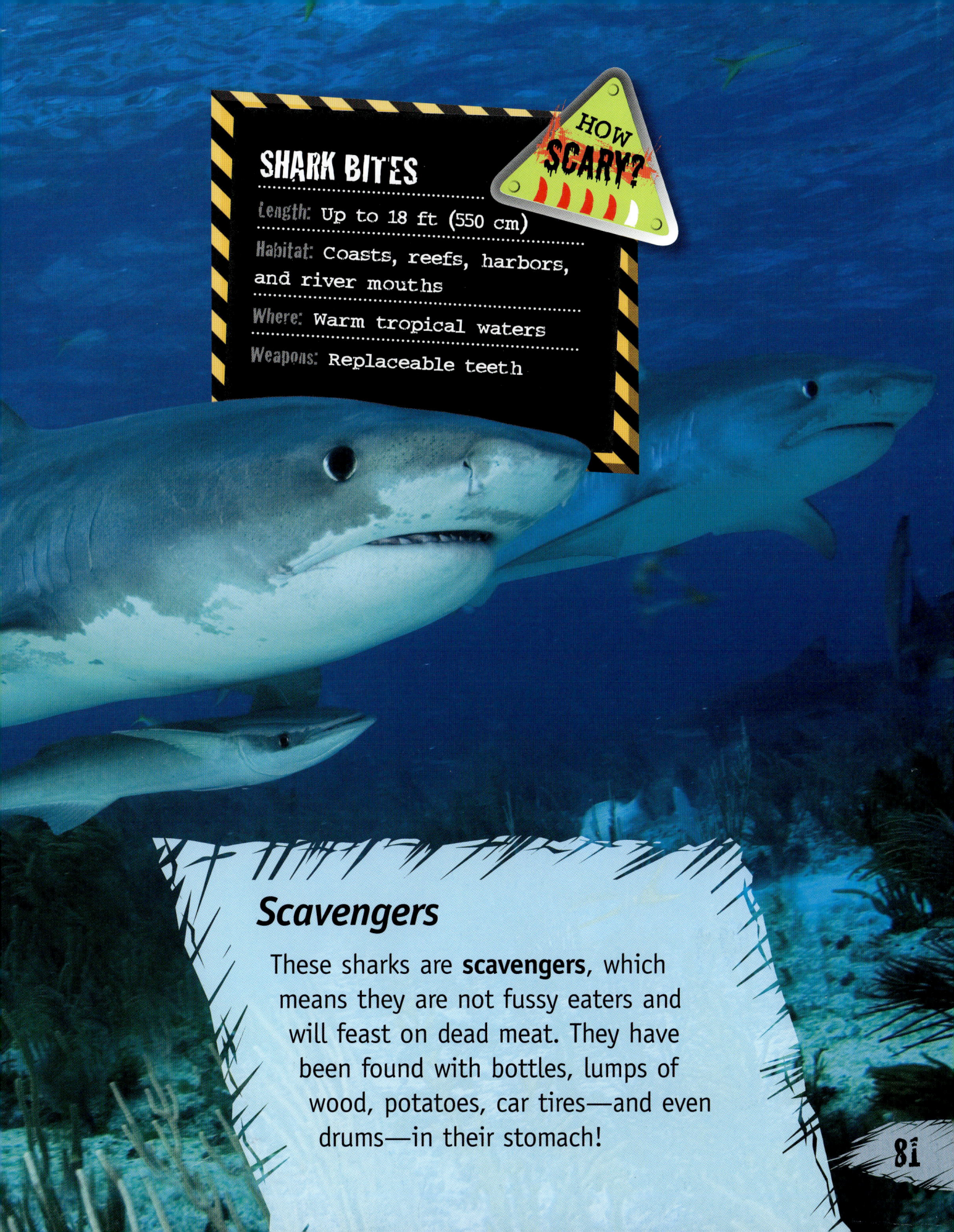

SHARK BITES

Length: Up to 18 ft (550 cm)

Habitat: Coasts, reefs, harbors, and river mouths

Where: Warm tropical waters

Weapons: Replaceable teeth

HOW SCARY?

Scavengers

These sharks are **scavengers**, which means they are not fussy eaters and will feast on dead meat. They have been found with bottles, lumps of wood, potatoes, car tires—and even drums—in their stomach!

FUNNEL-WEB SPIDER

16 Funnel-web spiders have glossy, brown, or black bodies, and do not look all that scary. But looks can be deceiving ...

A funnel-web spider waits in its tunnel for a tasty treat to pass by.

DEADLY BITES

Length: 1.2 in. (3 cm)

Habitat: Homes, yards, and forests

Where: Southeast Australia

Weapons: Enormous fangs

HOW SCARY?

Hidden from View

Funnel web spiders hide in dark, damp places. They live in burrows and weave silken trip lines around the entrances. When a little creature walks on the silk thread, the spider feels the vibrations and leaps out of its burrow to attack.

The venom affects the **nervous systems** of humans and monkeys, but not other mammals.

KILLER FACT

Funnel-web spiders can't swim, but they can stay alive in water for up to 30 hours.

Of all funnel-web spiders, the most dangerous are male Sydney funnel-web spiders, which have such deadly venom they can kill their prey in seconds. They have fangs nearly 0.4 in. (1 cm) long.

When it is time to mate, male Sydney funnel-web spiders come out of their burrows to look for females. They search relentlessly, and attack anyone who gets in their way.

83

KILLER WHALE

15 There is one predator that even a great white shark fears—the killer whale, or orca. These marine mammals are easy to spot, with their striking black and white markings.

KILLER FACT
Killer whales chase their prey at speed, reaching 35 mph (56 km/h), and even leap out of the air when they are in pursuit.

Teamwork

Killer whales often live and travel in groups called pods. They work as a team to catch their prey. Some pods just eat fish, while others prefer to hunt seals or other whales.

Killer whales are very daring in their hunting. Some even risk **beaching** themselves to snatch seals from the shoreline.

A killer whale tries to grab a sea lion from the beach. The whale must be very careful not to get stuck.

Killer whales are successful hunters because they have a range of hunting strategies and prey on many types of animal. Dolphins, whales, sharks, turtles, seals, and fish all have good reason to be afraid of killer whales!

DEADLY BITES

Length: 29.5 ft. (9 m)

Habitat: Ocean

Where: Worldwide

Weapons: Tail, head, and teeth

HOW SCARY?

BROWN RECLUSE SPIDER

14 Brown recluse spiders may be small, but they are fanged, fast-moving, eight-legged predators.

The pedipalps are short limbs on either side of the head.

Brown recluse spiders use special legs, called pedipalps, to grab and hold their prey while they inject venom with fangs. The bite of a brown recluse is usually painless to a human, but within a few hours a sore wound develops, which needs to be treated by a doctor.

KILLER FACT

Brown recluse spiders have a violin-shaped marking on their bodies, and are sometimes called violin spiders.

This spider's venom works by eating away at the skin, and can cause death in some people.

Most spiders have eight eyes, but brown recluse spiders have six. They build large, sticky webs that look like silken sheets, and often make their homes in dark corners of houses. They use their webs to hold their egg sacs, not to catch prey, which they hunt at night.

DEADLY BITES

Length: 0.6 in. (15 mm)
Habitat: Mostly tropical areas
Where: Worldwide
Weapons: Sharp fangs and a skin-eating venom

HOW SCARY?

TAIPAN

KILLER FACT
A taipan has enough venom to kill 250,000 mice, 150,000 rats—or 100 people!

13 Snakes are smooth-scaled, slithering predators. These reptiles have speed and super senses, and some can inject a deadly venom using their fearsome fangs.

The taipan is also called the "fierce snake."

The deadly taipan lives in Australian deserts and is the most venomous snake in the world. Taipans belong to a group of snakes that are called elapids.

Like most snakes, taipans hunt small animals to eat, even entering their burrows. They only attack people if they are feeling scared.

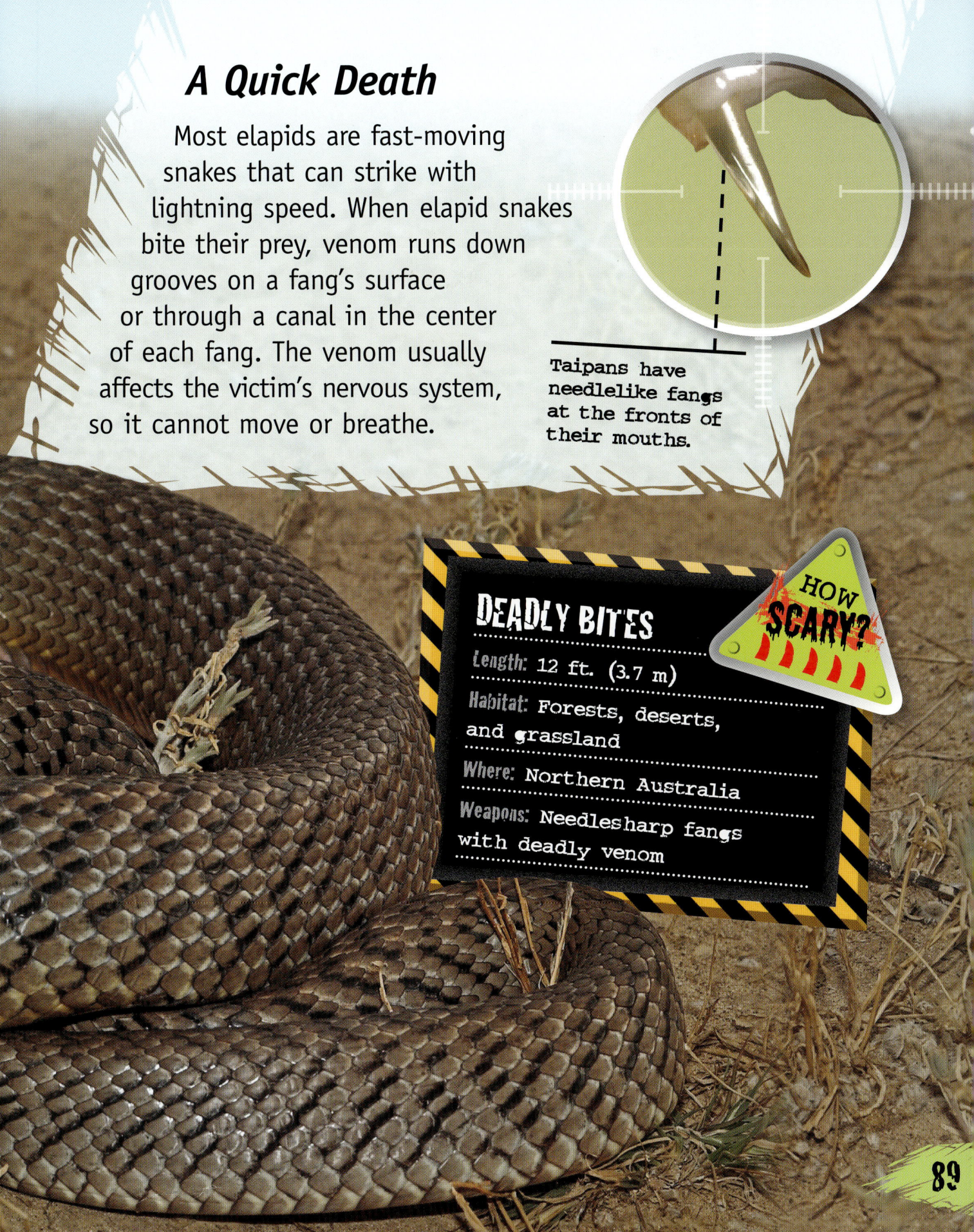

A Quick Death

Most elapids are fast-moving snakes that can strike with lightning speed. When elapid snakes bite their prey, venom runs down grooves on a fang's surface or through a canal in the center of each fang. The venom usually affects the victim's nervous system, so it cannot move or breathe.

Taipans have needlelike fangs at the fronts of their mouths.

DEADLY BITES

Length: 12 ft. (3.7 m)

Habitat: Forests, deserts, and grassland

Where: Northern Australia

Weapons: Needlesharp fangs with deadly venom

HOW SCARY?

ALLIGATOR

12 American alligators were so heavily hunted by humans for their skins, that they were in danger of dying out completely. Today, these impressive predators are protected.

This alligator is hiding under the algae, waiting for unsuspecting prey to pass by.

Killer Fact
Although they breathe air, alligators can stay underwater for up to six hours at a time.

Like other reptiles, alligators need to keep warm to move at speed, so they spend most of the day floating in water and **basking** in the sun. When they float, alligators can stay almost completely motionless. Just their eyes and the tips of their noses poke above the water—looking for prey and smelling the air.

SCORPION

11 The huge imperial scorpion has powerful pincers to kill its prey. Smaller, weaker scorpions rely on venomous stings to defeat their victims.

DEADLY BITES

Length: 8 in. (20 cm)
Habitat: Hot, dark, and dry places
Where: Worldwide
Weapons: Powerful claws and a venom-filled stinger

HOW SCARY?

The imperial scorpion holds the record as the world's largest scorpion.

Actual size!

Powerful muscles snap an alligator's jaws shut tight when it bites its prey. However, the muscles that open the jaws are much weaker, and an adult human is strong enough to hold an alligator's jaws shut.

Alligators usually eat smaller prey that they can kill in one bite, such as fish or turtles, but they will also attack large animals, such as deer or dogs.

DEADLY BITES

Length: 16.4 ft (5 m)
Habitat: Coasts, mangrove swamps, rivers, and lakes
Where: United States
Weapons: 74–80 teeth

HOW SCARY?

TURN THE PAGE TO GET UP-CLOSE TO A **DEADLY** ALLIGATOR!

Smaller young alligators often gather together in large groups.

Actual size!

Baby alligators are just 8.7 in. (22 cm) long when they hatch.

Taking Care

Female alligators build huge nests and lay about 45 eggs at a time. After the baby alligators hatch, their mother carefully lifts them in her mouth and takes each one down to the water.

Female scorpions give birth to live young and carry the babies on their backs.

10 An emperor scorpion can grow to 8 inches (20 cm) long. Its claws are covered with hairs that help this predator sense the movement of small animals nearby. It has strong pincers to grab and crush its prey, and only uses its venomous sting to attack large animals or to defend itself.

Death Stalker

9 Death stalker scorpions have large pincers, but these are too weak to hold their prey, such as insects, for long. When a scorpion has been successful in a hunt, it must quickly deliver a deadly blow. It bends its long tail over its head, and plunges the sharp, curved sting into its victim.

KILLER FACT

Death stalker scorpions are very aggressive, and can deliver lethal venom to humans.

RATTLESNAKE

8 If you hear the distinctive noise of a rattlesnake shaking its tail, you know it's time to escape—fast! These are supreme hunting serpents with speed, strength, and some unbelievable superskills.

Actual size!

The snake's rattle is at the end of its tail

Rattlesnakes spend most of the day sunbathing, or hiding under rocks and in burrows. They hunt at dusk, when small mammals come out to find food, and can strike with amazing speed.

DEADLY BITES

Length: Up to 6.6 ft. (2 m)
Habitat: Deserts, mountains, and scrubland
Where: Southern USA and Mexico
Weapons: Long, hinged fangs, and venom

HOW SCARY?

When a snake flicks its tongue, it is smelling and tasting the air. When the snake pulls its tongue back into its mouth, it senses the smell using a special organ in the roof of its mouth.

KILLER FACT
The Western diamondback is the most dangerous of all rattlesnakes, and its bites can prove deadly to humans.

Seeing in the Dark

Rattlesnakes can hunt in total darkness. They use special heat-detecting pits to find small animals. This super sense helps the snake to build up a picture of where an animal is, its size, shape, and even its movements.

Heat-detecting pit

PUFF ADDER

The body is thick, with a **girth** of up to 16 in. (40 cm).

7 When a puff adder is feeling scared, it puffs out its body to make itself look larger and hisses. But this snake has little to fear from anyone—it is one of Africa's deadliest snakes.

KILLER FACT
Puff adders are responsible for nearly two-thirds of all snakebites in Africa.

Puff adders are the most common snakes in Africa, and often live close to humans. They kill more people in Africa than any other kind of snake.

The pattern on its skin keeps the snake well hidden.

DEADLY BITES

Length: 39 in. (100 cm)
Habitat: Grassland and scrubland
Where: Central and southern Africa
Weapons: Ambushing skills, enormous fangs, and deadly venom

HOW SCARY?

Hiding

With brown and cream camouflage, puff adders can hide in the undergrowth, waiting to ambush small animals. Their large, heavy bodies slither silently between plants, but when prey is close, these cumbersome snakes turn into speedy hunters. If they encounter a human, puff adders can easily deliver enough venom to kill.

A puff adder's long fangs can pierce leather!

ON THE MOVE

A pointed nose and a streamlined body help a shark to swim fast.

Moving through water is harder work than moving through air. Most fish have a **streamlined** body shape, which means their body moves through water easily. So fast swimmers usually have a long, slender shape.

Most sharks move quickly through water, and their body is packed with powerful muscles. The world's fastest shark is the shortfin mako. It is thought that this shark may reach speeds of 53 miles (88 kilometers) per hour—that's about the same speed as a cheetah chasing its prey.

Pectoral fins control direction and movements up and down.

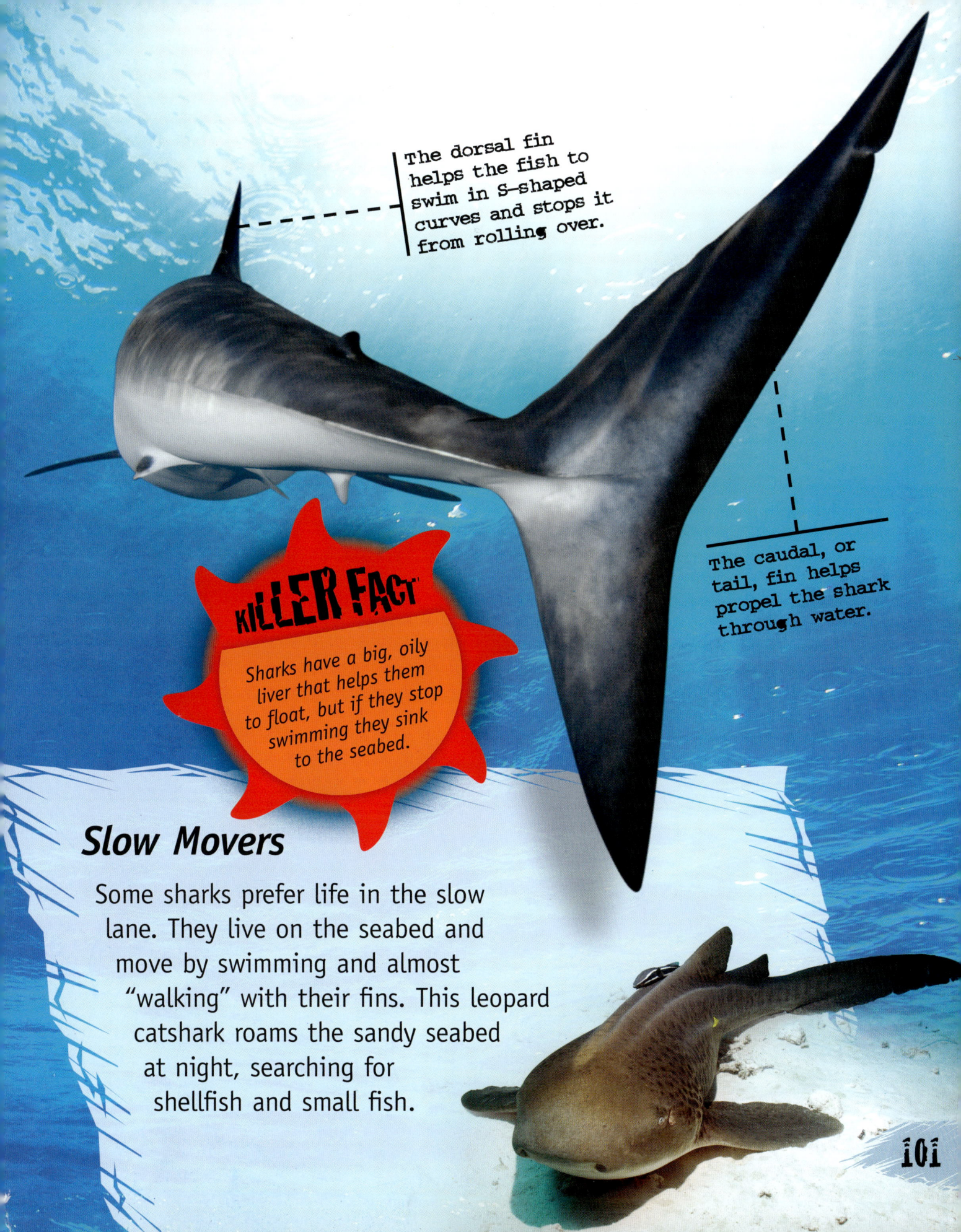

The dorsal fin helps the fish to swim in S-shaped curves and stops it from rolling over.

The caudal, or tail, fin helps propel the shark through water.

KILLER FACT

Sharks have a big, oily liver that helps them to float, but if they stop swimming they sink to the seabed.

Slow Movers

Some sharks prefer life in the slow lane. They live on the seabed and move by swimming and almost "walking" with their fins. This leopard catshark roams the sandy seabed at night, searching for shellfish and small fish.

BULL SHARK

6 This broad, strong shark is known for its aggressive nature. Bull sharks are described as "short tempered," which means they are always ready for a fight!

Bull sharks usually live and hunt on their own.

Almost all sharks live in seas and oceans, where the water is salty. Bull sharks are more adaptable. They live in shallow coastal waters, but they also swim up rivers, and have even been found in freshwater lakes. Spotting a bull shark can be difficult, because they often swim in cloudy water.

KILLER FACT

Some experts believe that the bull shark is the deadliest shark in the world.

DEADLY BITES

Length: Up to 11 ft (340 cm)
Habitat: Coasts, rivers, and bays
Where: Warm tropical waters
Weapons: Very aggressive, rapid acceleration, razor-sharp teeth

HOW SCARY?

Lateral line

Sensitive Senses

Bull sharks have poor eyesight. Instead, they rely on a superb sense of smell. Like other sharks, they have a sensitive line that runs along their body, called the lateral line. This detects movement and vibrations in the water.

SHARKS AND PEOPLE

Humans are much more deadly than sharks. It is rare for sharks to attack people, and most of those human victims do survive an attack. People, however, kill up to 120 million sharks every year.

Many of these majestic marine predators are now in grave danger of becoming extinct. That means they will disappear from our planet forever. Sharks are fished from the seas for their meat and their fins, which are used in soup. They are also caught accidentally by fishermen who are hoping to catch other fish to eat.

This dogfish died after getting tangled in a fisherman's net.

Shark cages allow scientists to study sharks close-up, without either the divers or the sharks getting into trouble.

Saving Sharks

We need sharks in our seas. They are part of the ocean ecosystem, and they play an important part in keeping the oceans healthy and in balance. We can help by not buying shark products, and by learning as much as we can about these beautiful fish.

KILLER FACT

There used to be ten times as many sharks in the oceans as there are today.

LION

DEADLY BITES
Length: 8.2 ft. (2.5 m) long
Habitat: African grasslands
Where: Central and southern Africa
Weapons: Massive teeth and claws

HOW SCARY?

5 Lions are unusual big cats. Like most predators, they have deadly weapons to catch and kill their prey. Unlike most predators, lions hunt in groups.

Even friendly, **tame** lions can suddenly turn on a human and decide it's time to eat!

Lions are strong and smart. They have superb senses of sight and smell, which help them to find antelope and zebras. They live and hunt in family groups called prides.

KILLER FACT
Lion hunts are most successful on moonless nights. In the dark, prey can't see the lions **stalking** them.

Lionesses do most of the hunting. They stalk their prey, creeping up close until it is time for the kill. They share the meat with the pride. An adult male can eat up to 95 lb. (43 kg) at one time—the weight of a 13-year-old child!

Actual size!

canine tooth

2 in. (5 cm)

Reasons to Kill

Hunting for food is hard work, but it's worth the effort. Meat is packed with energy, so a predator only needs to eat occasionally. In contrast, animals that eat plants need to spend most of their time feeding to get enough energy to live.

POLAR BEAR

KILLER FACT
A polar bear needs to kill up to 75 seals every year to survive.

4 Brown bears and polar bears are the world's largest land meat-eaters. Brown bears have a fearsome reputation, but they do not match polar bears' ruthless approach to hunting.

Polar bears eat most in the winter months, when they can hunt on the sea ice.

PREDATOR BITES

Length: 11.1 ft. (3.4 m)
Habitat: The ocean and icy regions
Where: Arctic and Northern Canada
Weapons: Sharp teeth and claws

HOW SCARY?

Polar bears are ferocious hunters and they rely almost entirely on a diet of meat from whales, dolphins, and seals. There are few plants in the Arctic so, unlike other bears, they cannot feed on berries or fruits.

Polar bears can survive for up to eight months without food. They are great swimmers, and can run as fast as a human for short stretches. A bear may walk as far as 3,100 miles (5,000 km) in just one year.

Actual size!

12 in. (30 cm)

Huge feet help bears walk on snow and swim quickly.

Seal Meal

To catch their favorite meal of seal, polar bears must wait by an ice hole, where seals pop up to breathe. A quick swipe with its massive claws and a snap of the jaws is all it takes to catch lunch.

SALTWATER CROCODILE

3 When the world's largest reptile decides it is hungry, no one is safe. The saltwater crocodile, or "saltie," is a fearsome hunter that uses stealth, speed, and strength to kill.

DEADLY BITES

Length: 8.2–23 ft. (2.5–7 m)

Habitat: Coasts, mangrove swamps, rivers, and lakes

Where: Southeast Asia to Australia

Weapons: 64–68 teeth

HOW SCARY?

Saltwater crocodiles live in warm waters in Asia and the Pacific Ocean. These massive crocodilians can grow to at least 16 feet (5 m) long, but it is thought that some males may grow to more than 23 feet (7 m) from snout to tail-tip. Despite their huge and heavy bodies, crocodiles can move with great speed on land and can outrun a human.

Salties hunt fish, mammals, and birds. They clamp their jaws around their prey and, gripping tightly, sink below the water. Then the crocodiles begin the "death roll," and spin their bodies until the prey is drowned.

Salties have 64–68 pointed teeth in their long jaws.

Actual size!

3.3 in. (8.5 cm)

Death Roll

Crocodiles can bite, but they can't chew. Their piercing teeth are perfect for grabbing hold of prey, but they might not kill it. That's why crocodiles perform a death roll.

KILLER FACT
Crocodiles sometimes hunt in groups, which suggests they are smarter than most reptiles.

MOSQUITO

2 At their best, mosquitoes are buzzing, biting bloodsuckers. At their worst, these flies are among the world's most dangerous pests.

Male mosquitoes mostly feed from flowers, but females have to feed on blood before they can lay their eggs. They search out mammals and birds to attack, and have long mouthparts that pierce skin.

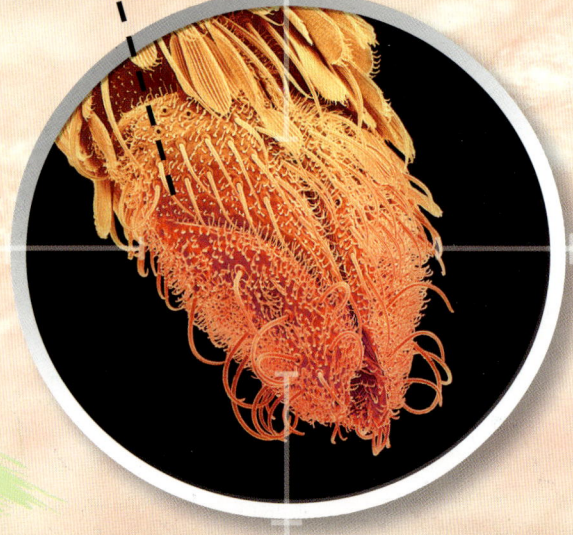

The tip of the mouthpart is needle-sharp.

As they break the skin, mosquitoes inject saliva to stop blood from clotting so they can keep sucking it up. Mosquitoes are parasites, and the animals they feed upon are called **hosts**.

- There are an estimated 10,000,000,000,000,000 ants in the world, and most of them can bite or sting!

- A killer whale hits seals with its head or thumps them with its tail to kill them.

- There are nearly 400 different types of shark, but only about 12 of them are dangerous to humans.

- Some crocodiles can gallop, chasing their prey at up to 11 miles (17 km).

- Bird-eating spiders shoot stinging hairs at their victims, causing intense pain.

- A polar bear can kill an adult walrus that is more than twice its size.

- The smallest shark in the world, the dwarf lanternshark, grows to just 7.8 in. (20 cm) long.

- About 2.5 million people are bitten by snakes every year.

- Funnel-web spider venom is deadly to humans and monkeys, but not to most other animals.

- Wolverines often steal the kills of smaller predators such as foxes.

TAKING IT FURTHER

What makes a creature "scary?" Now it's time for you to decide.

- Choose some scary features, such as speed, size, weapons (such as teeth, claws, or jaws), aggressive personality, favorite food, and special powers (such as venom or camouflage).

- Use this book, and the Internet, to award up to five points for each of the animal's scary features. Repeat for as many animals as you want.

- Turn your results into a table, graph or chart. Add up the totals to get a "Scary Score" for each deadly creature.

USEFUL WEBSITES

www.sharktrust.org
Discover more about the interesting world of sharks.

www.flmnh.ufl.edu/fish/sharks
A great website for finding up-to-date information on sharks.

ocean.nationalgeographic.com/ocean
For facts and photos about sharks and their habitat.

crocodilian.com
Plenty of information on crocodiles, alligators and caimans.

www.reptilegardens.com
An introduction to reptiles of all types and sizes.

www.sciencedaily.com
For the latest exciting news on science from around the world.

venomous-spiders.nanders.dk/spiderpictures.htm
Research lots more deadly spiders, in creepy close-up.

www.zsl.org/kids
Enjoy animal games, books and funny facts.

www.biology4kids.com/files/invert_main.html
Discover more invertebrates at this fact-packed website.

kids.nationalgeographic.com/kids
A great site for exploring the natural world.

www.kidsbiology.com
This website has a database of hundreds of animals.

www.bigcats.com
Play games and see amazing photos of big cats.

www.bears.org
Are all bears deadly? You can find out here.

gowild.wwf.org.uk
The World Wildlife Fund looks after animals and their homes.

www.arkive.org
Essential information on endangered animals.

GLOSSARY

alpha pair
A male and female pair that are the dominant animals in a group such as a pack of wolves.

ambush
A surprise attack made by an animal that has been lying hidden from view.

antivenom
A medicine that destroys deadly venom in a person's body.

bacteria
Tiny life forms that are too small to see with the naked eye. Bacteria are found wherever there is life on Earth.

basking
Lying in a warm place, such as sunlight, in order to get warm.

beaching
When a sea animal, such as a whale, becomes stranded on land.

binocular
Seeing using both eyes together. Binocular vision is good for hunting.

camouflage
A pattern of colors on an animal's body that hides it from predators or prey.

cannibals
Animals that eat others from the same species.

capybara
A large rodent that lives in the grasslands of South America.

cartilage
A strong, flexible fiber in animals' bodies. Sharks' skeletons are made from cartilage.

clotting
The process by which blood thickens after a wound has been made.

colony
A large group of animals living closely together.

constrictor
A kind of snake that kills its prey by squeezing it to death.

courtship
A series of rituals, such as flying displays, that animals perform to select a mate.

denticles
Hard scales on a shark's skin that help it to swim faster.

extinct
A species of animal that is no longer alive.

fangs
Long, pointed teeth that animals use for biting and tearing flesh.

freshwater
Water without salt in it, such as that found in lakes and rivers.

gills
Organs used by fish to breathe. The gills collect oxygen that is dissolved in the water.

girth
The distance around a body. The thicker its body, the bigger its girth.

gorge
To eat a huge amount of food at one time.

hosts
Animals that parasites such as mosquitoes feed on.

hatch
The breaking out of a baby animal from its egg.

invertebrates
Animals such as insects and spiders that do not have a backbone.

larvae
The young of animals such as insects, which change shape completely when they become adults.

marsupial
A kind of mammal, such as a kangaroo or a Tasmanian devil, that gives birth to very small young, which grow in a protective pouch in their mother's body.

mating
When a male and a female animal come together to reproduce.

nervous system
A network of nerve cells in an animal's body that carries signals to and from the brain.

paralyze
To stop a part of an animal's body from moving or feeling pain.

parasites
Animals or plants that feed on other animals or plants, called hosts. Parasites often cause their hosts harm.

plankton
Small animals and plants that float in the oceans, carried along by the ocean currents.

predators
Animals that hunt other animals to eat.

prey
Animals that are hunted by predators.

pup
The young of a shark.

radar
A system that uses radio waves to detect objects. The system gives off radio waves, then senses any waves that bounce back off objects in their way.

saliva
A liquid made inside an animal's mouth.

scavenger
An animal that feeds on dead animals or plants that it finds. Some sharks are scavengers.

segments
Parts of an animal's body that are similar to each other.

123

sensors
Organs in an animal that respond to stimuli such as light or magnetism.

serrations
A series of sharp points that make a sawlike cutting edge.

shed
To take off the outer layer of skin. Snakes shed their skin as they grow.

solitary
Living alone, away from other members of the same species.

species
A kind of animal or plant. Members of the same species are able to breed, producing young.

stalking
A method of hunting in which a predator follows its prey very quietly. When it gets up close to the prey, it attacks.

stealth
Moving carefully and quietly in order to sneak up on prey.

streamlined
A smooth shape that allows fluids such as water to flow easily around it.

stun
To knock an animal out suddenly.

suffocate
To die due to lack of oxygen, caused by not being able to breathe.

talons
The sharp claws of birds of prey.

tame
Not afraid of friendly humans.

toxins
Poisonous substances made in the bodies of some animals, which the animals use to attack other animals.

venom
A harmful substance that an animal injects into its victim's body by biting or stinging.

INDEX

allergies 40
alligator 90–91, 92–93
alligator snapping turtle 14–15
alpha pairs 74
Amazon River 20
ambush 49, 53, 64, 70, 99
ampullae of Lorenzini 9
anaconda 64–65
anti-venom 59
ants 22–25, 40–41
army ant 22–25
assassin bug 70–71
Australian redback spider 77

bacteria 44, 113
barbels 8
barbs 33
basking 90
basking shark 6–7
bats 18–19
beaching 84
bears 108–109
bees 32–33, 40, 50
beetles 11, 24
big cats 51, 60–63, 106–107
binocular vision 57
bird-eating spider 68–69
birds of prey 16–17, 50
bites 12, 13, 14, 24, 40, 63, 69, 71, 76, 89, 114, 115
bivouacs 23
black caiman 66–67
black widow spider 76–77
blood clotting 44, 112

blood suckers 18, 19, 44, 45, 70, 71, 112
blue shark 35
boas 64
bony fish 78
brown bear 108
brown recluse spider 86–87
bull shark 102–103
bulldog ant 40
bullet ant 41
burrows 13, 29, 59, 82, 88
butterfly fish 47

camouflage 42, 60, 79, 99
cannibals 39, 57
cartilage 78
caterpillars 42–43
catshark 39
caudal fins 101
centipedes 11
Chagas disease 70, 71
chimpanzee 48–49
claws 11, 53, 95
coastal sharks 36, 102
colonies 22, 23
colors, warning 13, 43, 58
constrictor snakes 64–65
cooperative hunting 49, 75, 84, 106, 111, 115
coral reefs 46, 47
coral snake 58–59
courtship 17, 77
crocodilians 50, 66–67, 90–93, 110–111
cubs 74

death roll 111
death stalker scorpion 95
dengue fever 113
denticles 79
diseases 44, 70, 71, 113
dogfish 104
dorsal fins 101

eels 20–21
eggs 28, 29, 38, 39, 45, 67, 91
elapids 88–89
electric eel 20–21
electricity 9, 20, 21
emperor scorpion 95
enamel 79
endangered animals 57
extinction 57, 66, 104
eyes 11, 35, 36, 56, 87
eyesight 36, 40, 56, 66, 103, 106

fangs 29, 68, 69, 83, 86, 88, 89, 99
feeding frezny 24
fins 100, 101
fire ant 41
fish 6–9, 20–21, 30–31, 34–39, 46–47, 56–57, 78–81, 100–105, 114–117
frilled shark 34
funnel-web spider 82–83

Gila monster 12–13
gills 7

goliath bird-eating spider
   68–69
gorge 61
great white shark 114–117
grey reef shark 46–47

hammerhead shark 56–57
hatch 67
hearing 75
heat-detecting pits 97
heat-sensing 18, 97, 113
hissing 55, 68, 98
honey badger 50–51
honeyguide bird 51
hornets 33
hosts 112
howling 75
humans, attacks on 24, 35,
   40, 43, 46, 55, 59, 66,
   77, 83, 86, 87, 95, 97,
   98, 104

imperial scorpion 94
invertebrates 10–11

jaws 21, 22, 31, 63, 72, 73,
   75, 93, 111
jumper ant 40–41

killer bee 32–33
killer whale 84–85
king cobra 54–55
kissing bug 71
Komodo dragon 52–53

kraits 29

larvae 45
lateral line 103
lemon shark 36–37, 38–39
leopard catshark 101
lion 51, 106–107
lioness 107
live birth 27, 28, 38, 65, 95
lizards 12–13, 17, 43, 52–53,
   58, 68
longnose sawshark 8–9
lonomia 42–43
lure 15

magnetic sensors 36
malaria 113
mallethead shark 56
mamba 55
mammals 13, 19, 27, 58, 61,
   66, 71, 83, 84, 97, 111,
   112
marsupials 27
mating 29, 69, 76, 77, 83
mermaid's purse 39
Mexican beaded lizard 13
milk 19
milk snake 59
mimicry 59
monkeys 49, 61, 83
Moray eel 21
mosquito 112–113
moths 19, 42
muscles 9, 29, 59, 100

nests 23, 91
nostrils 56, 66

orca *see* killer whale

packs 74
paralysis tick 44–45
parasites 44, 112
pectoral fins 100
pedipalps 86
pincers 41, 94, 95
piranha 30–31
plankton 6, 7, 34
pods 84
polar bear 108–109
possums 27
predators 11, 13, 14, 18, 20,
   22, 27, 34, 38, 42, 43, 48,
   50, 52, 55, 56, 58, 60, 66,
   67, 68, 70, 72, 74, 80, 84,
   86, 88, 90, 95, 104, 106,
   107, 114
prey 6, 8, 9, 11, 13, 16, 17,
   18, 19, 20, 21, 24, 29, 31,
   36, 40, 45, 47, 49, 51, 53,
   55, 56, 57, 60, 61, 64, 65,
   70, 71, 72, 75, 83, 84, 85,
   86, 87, 89, 94, 95, 99,
   106, 107, 111, 113, 114,
   115
prides 106, 107
puff adder 98–99
pups 38, 39
pythons 50, 64

127

raptors 16–17, 50
rattlesnake 96–97
remoras 37
reptiles 12–15, 28–29, 52–55, 58–59, 64–65, 88–89, 90–91, 96–99, 110–111
rostrum 8

saltwater crocodile 110–111
saws 8, 9
scavengers 27, 33, 37, 73, 81
scorpions 10, 24, 94–95
scutigera 10–11
sea snake 28–29, 80
seals 80, 84, 109
secretary bird 16–17
segments 11
shark cages 105
sharks 6–9, 34–39, 46–47, 56–57, 78–81, 100–105, 114–117
sharksuckers 37
shoals 30, 31
shortfin mako shark 100
Siberian tiger 61
skin shedding 29
skin trade 66, 90
smell, sense of 27, 60, 66, 75, 103, 106
snakes 16, 17, 28–29, 50, 54–55, 58–59, 64–65, 80, 88–89, 96–99
social insects 23
solitary animals 46, 60, 102
speed 16, 18, 34, 60, 84, 88, 89, 90, 96, 97, 100, 109, 111, 115, 117
spiders 10, 24, 68–69, 70, 76–77, 82–83, 86–87
spines 42, 43
squid 8, 35, 47, 80
stalking 63, 106
stealth 60, 110
stingrays 56, 80
stings 33, 40, 41, 94, 95
streamlined body shape 100
swarms 32
swell shark 78–79
Sydney funnel-web spider 83

taipan 88–89
talons 16
Tasmanian devil 26–27
teeth 8, 19, 21, 30, 31, 48, 53, 80, 111, 115
termite nests 49
territories 60
ticks 44–45
tiger 60–63
tiger shark 80–81
tongues 12, 19, 97
tool-makers 49
toxins 21, 45, 70
turtles 14–15, 66, 80, 93

underwater breathing 7

vampire bat 18–19
venom 11, 12, 13, 28, 29, 33, 40, 43, 44, 53, 55, 59, 69, 76, 83, 86, 87, 88, 89, 94, 95, 99

vibration detectors 103
violin spider see brown recluse spider

wallabies 27
wasps 33
webs 76, 87
Western diamondback rattlesnake 97
whale shark 34–35
wings 16, 19
wobbegong shark 79
wolf 74–75
wolverine 72–73

Made in the USA
Middletown, DE
22 February 2018

Thank You!

A book takes many people working together to make it a reality. So, to all the Kickstarter backers that helped me complete this project I wish to express a big 'Thank You', and I hope we can do more great things in the future.

Anthony Storms Akins
Alan Prak
Alessandro
Andy Lee
Bill Stull
Brandon Thompson
Charles Rogers
Clement Labadie
Demian Vonder Kuhlen
Edgar Rodriguez
Gordon
Greg_Vee
Gregory Pfrommer
Gregory R. Kinnicutt
J.T. O'Gara
Janakan

Jeff
Joe
Joshua Bauder
Marco Randall
Marshall Walker
Neer Patel
Nigel J Allen
Padrao
Perry Yap
R.C. Lewis
Randy Morris
Rowan Knight
Sebastian Lange
Shahid Ali Shah
Shrawan
Stan Spears

funded with KICKSTARTER

Credits & Legal

AUTHOR
Ivelin Demirov

EDITORS
Anton Berezin
Beth McMillan

PAGE DESIGN
Jordan Milev

ILLUSTRATOR
Ivelin Demirov

PROOFREADER
Beth McMillan

ACKNOWLEDGMENT
I must acknowledge the help of the online Python community, who have toiled in the background for many years to help make Python the exciting programming language it has become.

NOTICE OF RIGHTS
All rights reserved. No part of this book may be reproduced in any form, by any means without the written permission of the publisher or the author.

TRADEMARKS
All trademarks are held by their respective owners.

NOTICE OF LIABILITY
The information in this book is distributed on an "As Is" basis, without warranty. While every precaution has been taken in the preparation of the book, neither the author nor the publisher shall have any liability to any person or entity with respect to any loss or damage caused or alleged to be caused directly or indirectly by the instructions contained in this book or by the computer software and hardware products described in it.

PAPERBACK ISBN
ISBN-13: 978-1507727072
ISBN-10: 1507727070

COPYRIGHT
©2015 Ivelin Demirov

CONTACTS
pythonvisually.com

About this book

THE PROBLEM

People cannot be blamed for thinking programming is hard when trying it out for the first time. Learning to program is like learning a new language.

A number of rules and grammar syntax guidelines exist to follow. It also requires memorizing a bevy of glossary terms for each language, and unless a person works with programming at least 8 hours a day, the person is unlikely to become very familiar with programming quickly; at least, that has been the situation for years until now.

THE METHODOLOGY

Our approach involves teaching programming concepts via simple illustrations.

The visual approach works because it is one of the most fundamental ways of learning. Everyone as a baby and toddler learns the world around them via sight and sound long before there is comprehension associated with letters and meanings.

Programming works in modules and building blocks. As a person learns a few basic modules and steps, he can then learn to build more complex modules on those first basic units.

It's a building block approach where bigger structures can be coded once the basic modules are mastered. I start with a set of basic building blocks that are easy to learn through illustrations and metaphors.

From there, a user can apply multiple variations and build further. However, the initial set of building blocks becomes a Rosetta stone of sorts, allowing a user to program and build in any situation going forward.

Table of Contents

Why Python? 5
Installation 6
Hello World! 7
Part I: Built-in language features 10
Variables 11
Data types 16
Basic Math 19
String operations 28
Comments 35
Functions 37
If/Else and conditional statements 45
Classes and objects 55
Collections 63
Tuples 64
Lists 66
Loops 73
File operations 79
Exceptions 82
Part II: Standard Library 85
Import statement and Python modules and packages 86
File operations using os module 89
Regular Expressions 96
Math module 104
JSON 106
SQL: sqlite3 112
Part III: Popular 3rd party libraries 122
3rd party packages 123
Web Development with Flask 124
Recipes for task automation 130

When you embark on your computer science journey at college, you'll probably start by learning Python.

So why choose Python over any other programming language?
It's simple:

> Regardless of your operating system, Python is easy to set up.

> Python code uses plain English, making it easy to understand.

> Python will let you run bad code.
  Why is this good?
  When you're learning you're bound to make mistakes.
  Python tells you what the error is after you run the code, helping you to find the problem.

> Python is a very powerful tool, but it's also easy and fast to learn, which is why most people prefer it.

Installation

There are pre-compiled packages made for easy installation on multiple operating systems such as Windows, Linux, UNIX and Mac OS to name but a few.
If you head over to https://www.python.org/downloads/ you can select the right installation method for your operating system. Most Linux systems come with Python pre-installed.

Version 3 of Python is used in this book.
In Windows, once you have installed Python, select Python IDLE or Python command line/console from the Start menu or screen.

The difference between the IDLE and the console is that the IDLE has a graphical interface, which looks similar to a text editor. In Linux, UNIX, and OS X, you can launch Python emulator from command line by typing Python.

To choose a specific version of Python type PythonX where X is the version number (e.g. "Python3" for version 3).

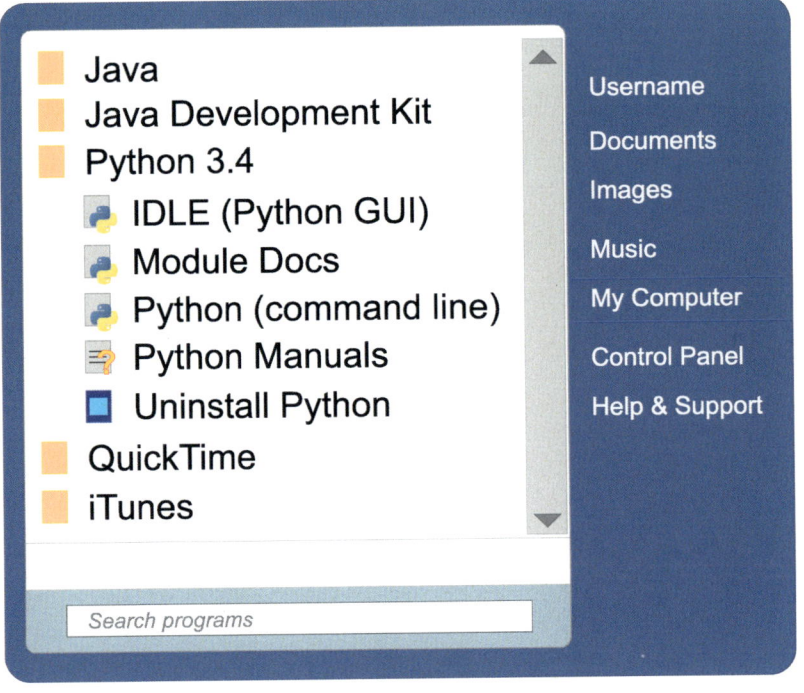

Most of the time that you write Python code, you will be writing the script in the IDLE or any other IDE like Eclipse or rich text editor like Sublime text or Notepad++. However, you can use the Python interpreter to write code interactively as it acts like a UNIX shell,

Even though it is possible to create programs using just the interpreter it is strongly recommended not to do so since it is hard to save the code as a script for further reuse. Rather consider the interpreter as an "on the fly" testing tool for your coding ideas.

Now lets make the interpreter output "Hello World!" string on the screen. Lets do it via the interpreter.

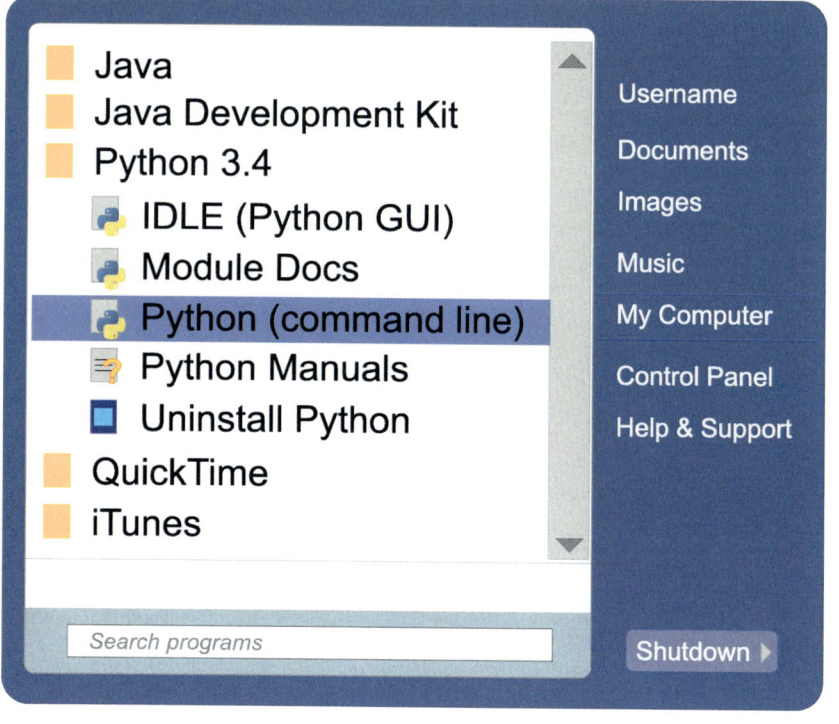

Terminal way

Launch the interpreter from command line using Python command as it was described in the previous chapter.

Type the following: `print("Hello world!")` and hit **"Enter"**.

The terminal shall look the following way:

```
C:\Python34\python.exe

Python 3.4.1
Type "help", "copyright", "credits" or "license" for
more information.
>>>print("Hello world!")
Hello world!
>>>
```

In the code snippet above you can see that the first line starts with `>>>`.
This symbol indicates the line where you provide dynamic input to the interpreter. Notice, as soon as the result of your first command was printed on the screen the interpreter printed `>>>` again. Giving instructions to the interpreter is sequential. You give one instruction - you wait till execution finishes, you enter another command and so on.

Note, further on in this book if you spot `>>>` symbol in a code snippet it shall mean that you are expected to test the code in the interpreter yourself.

On the first line you entered a statement. The statement is nothing else but an instruction for a computer to perform some task. The task could be anything from `make_a_coffee` to `launch_a_rocket`. In your case it is a simple print function though.
Functions will be covered further in this book.

One of the main principles of software engineering is reusability.
Let's make the code that was just tested in the interpreter reusable.

To do so, create a file called "hello_world.py" and type the following text inside:

```
1.  print("Hello World!")
```

What you placed into the file is exactly the line that was previously executed via the interpreter.

Now lets execute the script that you wrote.

Open the command line, navigate to the location where the script resides and type the following: python hello_world.py. After you hit enter you shall see that a "Hello World!" text was placed on the screen.

Congratulations!
You've managed to write your first Python program and successfully launch it.

Part I: Built-in language features

In Python, a variable can be used to store the output of a statement in the computer's memory.

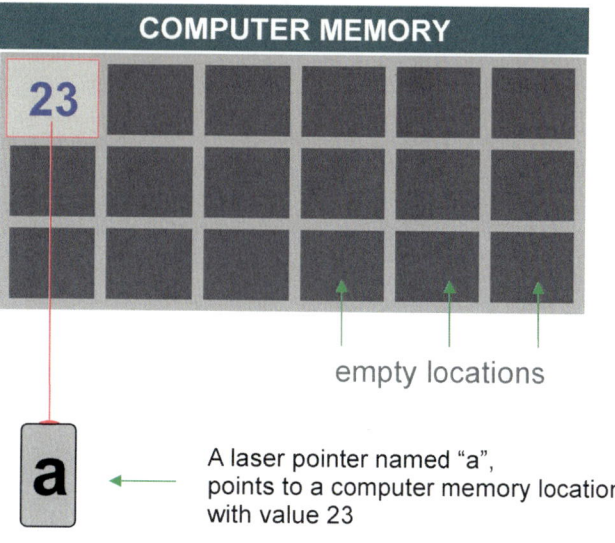

empty locations

A laser pointer named "a", points to a computer memory location with value 23

The *equals sign* is used to assign a value to a variable.
The name of the variable is called its identifier

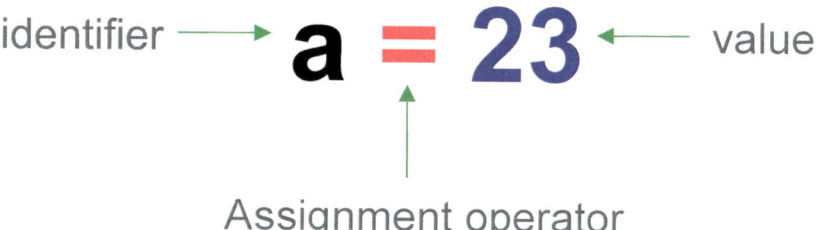

identifier → **a** = **23** ← value

Assignment operator

Variables

lets change the value of b from 11 to 8

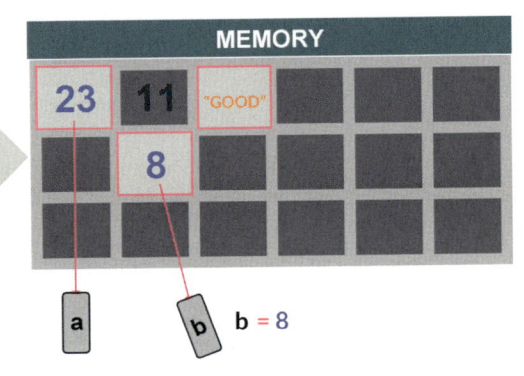

a = 23   b = 11   name ="GOOD"

b = 8

Because numbers are immutable, "b" changes location to the new value.
When there is no reference to a memory location the value fades away and the location is free to use again.
This process is known as garbage collection

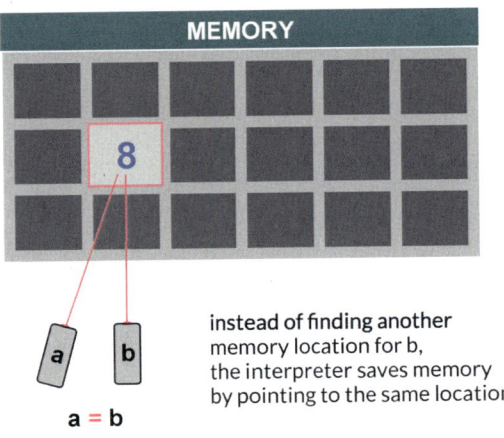

instead of finding another memory location for b, the interpreter saves memory by pointing to the same location

a = b

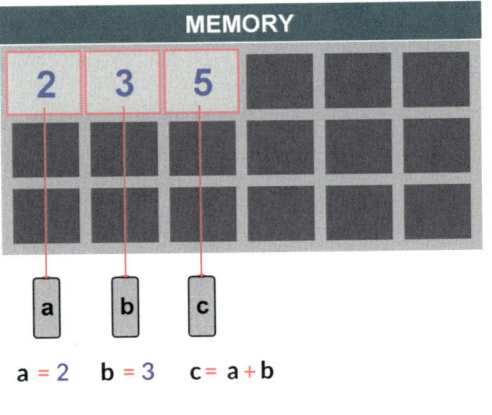

a = 2   b = 3   c = a + b

This is how to test if 'a' and 'b' share the same memory location

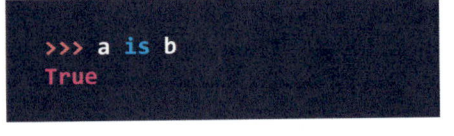

```
>>> a is b
True
```

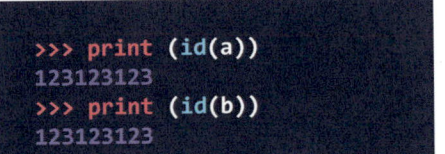

```
>>> print (id(a))
123123123
>>> print (id(b))
123123123
```

You may assign the same value to multiple variables using the following syntax:

```
>>> a = b = c = d = f = "Hello World!"
>>> a
Hello World!
>>> c
Hello World!
>>> f
Hello World!
```

Python variable names must follow the following rules:

1. They must start with a letter or an underscore
2. They must contain only letters, digits or underscores

Several examples of illegal variable names:

```
1. 2var
2. var-bar
3. foo.loo
4. @var
5. $var
```

Python also has some special words that can't be used as variable names:

```
and     assert   break   class    continue  def    del      elif
else    except   exec    finally  for              from   global   if
import  in       is      lambda   not              or     pass     raise
return  try      while   yield
```

Exercises

PROBLEM: Which statements are valid?

```
1.  $foo = "bar"

2.  lambda = "bar"

3.  finally = "yes"

4.  pass = "you shall not"

5.  ___buga_wuga_ = "@@@huz"

6.  foo_bar = "bar"
```

ANSWER: The two last ones. Note, the statement before the last one just looks incorrect. In reality it is a completely legal variable with a proper string value

Exercises

PROBLEM: Assign value "blah" to variables zen, foo and bar in one line.

YOUR CODE:

```
1
2
3
4
5
6
7
8
```

ANSWER:

```
foo = bar = zen = "blah"
```

Data types

```
item = group[ (current.index + 1 ) % len ];
```

| MUTABLE | IMMUTABLE |

NUMERIC

| Integer | | `integer = 3` |
| Float | | `my_float = 10.2` |

SEQUENCES

String		`text = "String"` `text2 = 'String2'`
Byte		`x = b'normal string'`
Byte Array		`y = bytearray(b"Hello World!")`
List		`myList = [1, 2, 3, 4, 5]`
Tuple		`myTuple = (a, b, c, d, e)`

SETS

| Set | | `a = set("Set")    # {'S', 'e', ' ', 't'}` |
| Frozen Set | | `b = frozenset(["Paris", "NY", "Milano"])` |

MAPPINGS

| Dictionary | | `employee = {name: "Joe", age: 21, id: 99}` |

18

The following table provides an overview of the most frequently used data types in Python.

Variable type	Example	Usage comment
bool	life_is_good = True hamsters_are_evil = False	true/false values
int, long	size_of_shoes = 42 earth_population = 7000000000	various whole digits
float	pi = 3.14159265359	not whole digits - with one or more signs after a dot
str	chinese_hi = "你好"	any text
None	my_new_book = None	empty variable without any meaningful value

You can store data of all types inside a variable using the assignment operator "=".

Multiline strings can be used to store large text blocks.

```
long_text = """ Line one
Line two
Line three
Line Four
"""
```

As you can see, a multiline string is a normal string enclosed by triple quotes instead of single ones.

In Python it is possible to convert strings to integers and integers to strings:

```
>>> str(100)
'100'
>>> int("234")
234
```

Quiz

PROBLEM:

1. What is the name of this = operator?

2. How to convert a digit 3.14 into a string '3.14'?

ANSWER:

1. assignment operator

2. `str(3.14)`

Python has a bunch of built-in arithmetic operators. The table below provides a brief comparison of the short notations and their longer equivalents.

Assume that initially the following is true: a = 3.

Operation name	Short notation	Long notation	Value of a	Comment
Addition	a += 1	a = a + 1	4	
Subtraction	a -= 1	a = a - 1	2	
Multiplication	a *= 2	a = a * 2	6	
Division	a /= 2	a = a / 2	1.5	Returns decimal values or float numbers
Modulo	a %= 2	a = a % 2	1	Returns an integer remainder of a division
Exponent	a **= 2	a = a ** 2	9	Similar to a^2 in regular maths
Floor division	a //= 2	a = a // 2	1	Returns only decimal (int) values
Negation	a = -a	a = 0 -a	-3	Returns the same value with an opposite sign

Finding the square root of a number is also easy in Python, but it's not a built-in language feature. You'll find out about it later in the book!

You can calculate the absolute value of a digit (e.g. |-3|), using abs(). For example, abs(-3) returns 3.

Operators precedence

The order of execution of mathematical operations in Python is similar to the order used in conventional mathematics.

In maths there are three general operator priority levels:

1. exponents and roots
2. multiplication, division and modulus
3. addition and subtraction

Exponents and roots are represented by functions of a standard library in Python and are covered further on in this book.

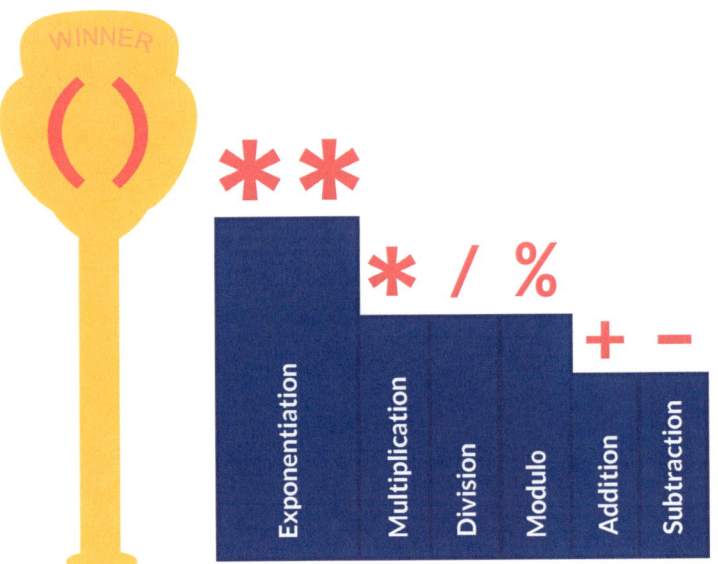

All other priority levels have their own built-in Python operators.

Higher order operations are performed before the lower ones. All the operations of the same order are executed one by one from left to right.

For example, the statement: 2 + 3 * 4 - 1 returns 13. The multiplication is performed before the addition and subtraction.

In order to affect the order of operator execution, you should use parentheses (). For example, (3 + 6) * 2 equals 18 and 8 / (1 + 1) equals 4.

22

The code snippet below shows how simple maths operations are processed in the Python interpreter.

```
>>> 13 * 2
26

>>> 10 - 32
-22

>>> 11 % 10
1

>>> 6 ** 2
36

>>> 12 / 8
1.5

>>> 12 % 8 + (12 // 8) * 8
12

>>> 6 - -16
22

>>> a = 16
>>> a += 3
>>> a
19

>>> a = 4
>>> b = 6
>>> a *= b
>>> a
24
```

Exercises

PROBLEM:

Try to answer the following questions without Python and then use the interpreter to verify your answers:

1. What is the result of the following calculation: *2 + 2 + 2 + 2 + 2 + 2 * 0?*

2. What about this one: *(2 + 2 + 3 + 4) * (4 * 4 - (2 * 6 + 4))?*

YOUR CODE:

```
1
2
3
4
5
6
7
8
```

ANSWER:

1. 10 - if you answered 0 you forgot that multiplication has a higher precedence than addition

2. 0 - if you answer was something else you forgot that operations in brackets should be performed first - a product of the second expression in brackets - *(4 * 4 - (2 * 6 + 4))* is 0 and anything multiplied by 0 is 0 as well

24

Exercises

PROBLEM: A car has a speed of 100 km/h. Write some code that calculates the distance in meters (not kilometers!) that the car would travel in N hours. Set N to 10.

YOUR CODE:

```
1
2
3
4
5
6
```

ANSWER:

```
1.  N = 10
2.  distance_in_kilometers = 100 * N
3.  distance_in_meters = distance_in_kilometers * 1000
```

Exercises

PROBLEM: Rewrite the code using short notations

```
1.  N = N * J
2.  i = i + j * 18
3.  f = f - k / 2
```

YOUR CODE:

```
1
2
3
4
5
6
```

ANSWER:

```
1.  N *= J
2.  i += j * 18
3.  f -= k / 2
```

Exercises

PROBLEM:

Given that f(x) = |x^3 - 20|, find f(-3). Your answer should consist of two lines of code: one which initialises x to -3, and one that calculates the result.

YOUR CODE:

```
1
2
3
4
5
6
```

ANSWER:

The following Python code shall do the job:

```
>>> x = -3
>>> abs(x ** 3 - 20)
47
```

Exercises

PROBLEM: Try to solve the previous problem using -3 inline, rather than using the x variable.

YOUR CODE:

```
1
2
3
4
5
6
```

ANSWER: Your solution should look like this:

```
>>> abs((-3) ** 3 - 20)
47
```

If it looks like this:

```
>>> abs(-3 ** 3 - 20)
47
```

it is wrong because negation (i.e. subtraction from zero) has lower precedence than the exponent and thus has to be enclosed in parentheses. Even though your solution gives the same result as the correct one, it is a pure coincidence. Try to find value of x for $f(x) = |x^2 - 20|$ with and without parentheses around the negation to see the difference.

Exercises

PROBLEM: How can you check if an integer is odd using Python?

YOUR CODE:

```
1
2
3
4
5
6
```

ANSWER: Use the modulo operator to find the remainder when you divide by 2.
If the remainder is 1, the digit is odd.

```
>>> 3 % 2
1

>>> 4 % 2
0
```

String operations

Words and sentences are collections of characters, and so are Python strings.

You can access any character in a Python string using its index, either counting from the beginning or the end of the string. When you start from the beginning, you count from 0.

name = "My Name is Mike"

M	y		N	a	m	e		i	s		M	i	k	e
0	1	2	3	4	5	6	7	8	9	10	11	12	13	14
-15	-14	-13	-12	-11	-10	-9	-8	-7	-6	-5	-4	-3	-2	-1

INDEXING

In Python integer indices are zero based.

```
>>> name = "My Name is Mike"
>>> name[0]
'M'
>>> name[1]
'y'
>>> name[9]
's'
>>> name[-1]
'e'
>>> name[-15]
'M'
>>> name[7]
' '
```

You can take shorter substrings from inside a longer string.
This operation is called 'slicing'.

```
>>> name[11:14]   # from 11th to 14th, 14th one is excluded
'Mik'
>>> name[11:15]   # from 11th to 15th, 15th one is excluded
'Mike'
```

If you want to check if a string contains
a particular substring, you can use the
'in' operator.

```
>>> "B" in "Foo"
False
>>> "B" not in "Foo"
True
>>> "G" in "Gohl"
True
>>> "James" in "James is tall"
True
```

The len function calculates the
length of a string.

```
>>> len(name)
15
```

31

Concatenation

In Python it's possible to combine two strings into one:

The operation is called *concatenation*.

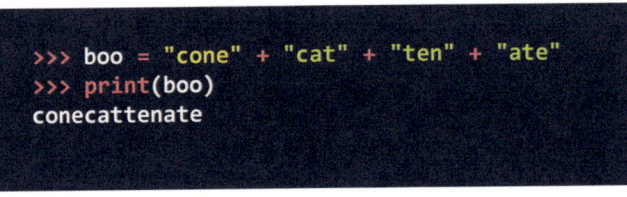

```
>>> boo = "cone" + "cat" + "ten" + "ate"
>>> print(boo)
conecattenate
```

```
>>> foo = "one"
>>> bar = "two"
>>> full = foo + " " + bar
>>> print(full)
one two
```

If you want a string containing N substrings, you use the * operator.

```
>>> foo = "foo " * 3
>>> print(foo)
foo foo foo
```

Quiz

PROBLEM:

1. In Python it is possible to combine multiple strings into one. What is the name of this operation?

2. There is a string $value$ = "foobar". You access a substring the following way:
   other_value = value[1:3].
   What is the name of this operation? How long is $other\_value$?

3. What is the index of the first character in a string?

ANSWER:

1. Concatenation

2. Slicing. The length is 2. The last character defined by slicing operation is not included.

3. 0

Exercises

PROBLEM:

There are two strings: one = "John is strong" two = "Tea is not warm".
Write Python code to produce a string result = "John is not strong" out of
one and two:

YOUR CODE:

```
1
2
3
4
5
6
```

ANSWER:

```
1.  result = one[0:8] + two[7:11] + one[8:14]
```

Exercises

PROBLEM: Find which of these strings doesn't contain the letter *"B"*: *"Foo"*, *"Bar"*, *"Zoo"*, *"Loo"*.

YOUR CODE:

```
1
2
3
4
5
6
```

ANSWER:

```
>>> "B" in "Foo"
False
>>> "B" in "Bar"
True
>>> "B" in "Zoo"
False
>>> "B" in "Loo"
False
```

Exercises

PROBLEM:

Use the Python interpreter to find the length of the string *"John is strong"*

YOUR CODE:

```
1
2
3
4
5
6
```

ANSWER:

```
>>> len("John is strong")
14
```

Writing comments on Python code is rather simple.
There are two ways to write Python comments, single line comments, and multiple line comments.

Comments are intended to help the user to understand the code, and are ignored by the interpreter.

Single line comments are created by adding the # character to the beginning. They are useful for adding small comments at the beginning of functions.

```
1.    # This is a valid single line comment.
```

You can also add inline comments after a line of code, which can be useful for clarifying statements.

```
1.  print("Hello there!")          # This would be an inline comment in Python
2.  # This is another.
```

Multi-line Comments

Rather than chaining several single line comments together, for larger comments, you can use three consecutive quotation marks on the first and last line.

```
1.  """ This is a better way
2.  of using  comments that span
3.  over multiple lines without
4.  having to use lots of hashes.
5.  """
```

This type of commenting is often used as documentation for anyone reading the program. After all, no matter how skilled you are, if you get a program with no comments, you will have to spend time checking the code to figure out what it does and how to use it unless you knew beforehand.

We talked before about how reusability is a key principle of software engineering. Once you've written some code, you'll want to store it so you can use it again without having to copy and paste.

This is what functions are for! Functions are a way to wrap up your code so it can be used again by calling an easy shortcut.

Let's say you want to be able to print *"Hello Mr. Jones! How are you today?"* three times in a row without any code duplication. This can be achieved in the following way:

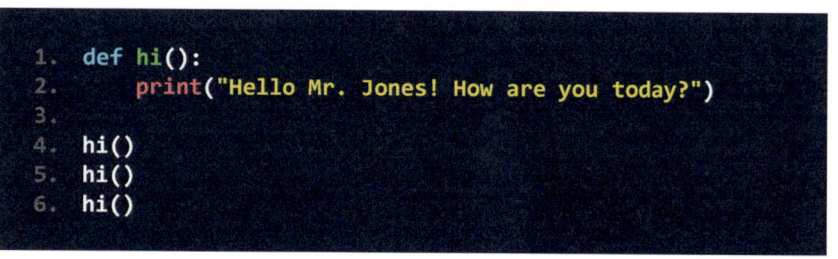

```
1.  def hi():
2.      print("Hello Mr. Jones! How are you today?")
3.
4.  hi()
5.  hi()
6.  hi()
```

Basic functions

In the code snippet above you can see the keyword "def". This defines a code block that represents the function. Function names have to follow the same rules as variable names. This function is called "hi", and is followed by parentheses and a colon. Inside the parentheses is the argument list, which in this case is completely empty.
After the function, the code block has to be indented to define it as a nested block.

There are two Python conventions you should stick to: use four spaces to indent your code blocks, and use only lowercase letters and underscores in function names.

This code would not work:

<non-indented example>

```
1.  def hi():
2.  print("Hello Mr. Jones! How are you today?")
```

This code would not work:

<inconsistent indentation>

```
1.  def hi():
2.          print("Hello Mr. Jones! How are you today?")
3.      print("foobar")
```

Below the function you may see three lines where it is invoked.
Lets have a look at one particular invocation:

```
1.  hi()
```

The invocation is just a function name followed by the arguments that are supposed to be passed as an argument list. The arguments are expected to be placed within brackets. In this case we have no argument list thus the brackets are empty.

Sometimes, you'll want functions to alter their behaviour in different conditions. To do this, you can use function arguments.

Let's say you want to say hi not just to Mr. Jones, but to a person with any name. You'll have to edit the original hi() function to look like this:

```
1.  def hi(name):
2.      print("Hello " + name + "! How are you today?")
```

The function now accepts a single argument, which is a variable called "name". Later, "name" is concatenated with two parts of the original string to give your new greeting.

Now you can say hi to John, James, and Maggie, like so:

```
1.  hi("John")
2.  hi("James")
3.  hi("Maggie")
```

This would sequentially print:

```
Hello John! How are you today?
Hello James! How are you today?
Hello Maggie! How are you today?
```

Note, instead of passing a value directly you can assign the value to a variable and pass the variable to the function.

```
1.  first_name = "John"
2.  hi(first_name)
```

Once you've set up the function to use an argument, trying to call it without supplying an argument will cause an error.

Default values

To avoid these errors, you can give your arguments default values, which can be overridden if needed.

```
1.  def hi(name="sir"):
2.      print("Hello " + name + "! How are you today?")
```

In this case you can call the function with and without the argument. Calling:

```
1.  hi()
2.  hi("James")
```

would print:

```
Hello sir! How are you today?
Hello James! How are you today?
```

Functions can have a mixture of arguments with default values and without. Those with default values have to come at the end of the argument list.

```
1.  def foo(bar, zoo="blah"):
2.      ...
```

is valid. Meanwhile:

```
1.  def foo(bar="blah", zoo):
2.      ...
```

is not.

42

Lets have a look at one of the code snippets that was covered previously in the exercises:

```
1.  N = 10
2.  distance_in_kilometers = 100 * N
3.  distance_in_meters = distance_in_kilometers * 1000
```

What if you want to encapsulate this logic in a function in such a manner that you could pass time in hours and speed in km/h and somehow get back a distance traveled in meters?

This logic could be implemented using the following function:

```
1.  def get_distance(speed, duration):
2.      distance_in_kilometers = speed * duration
3.      distance_in_meters = distance_in_kilometers * 1000
4.      return distance_in_meters
```

The function's last line contains a return statement. The best way to understand what it does is to have a look at several invocations of the function:

```
1.  speed = 100
2.
3.  initial_distance = get_distance(speed, 0)
4.  distance_after_a_day = get_distance(speed, 24)         # day is 24 hours
5.  distance_after_a_week = get_distance(speed, 24 * 7)    # week is 7 days
```

As you may have guessed, the return statement allows you to store the output of the function in a variable. After executing the lines above the variables shall have the following values:

variable	value
initial_distance	0
distance_after_a_day	2400000
distance_after_a_week	16800000

Exercises

PROBLEM:

There is a mathematical function f(x,y) = x^y + 100.
Implement the function in Python.

YOUR CODE:

```
1
2
3
4
5
6
```

ANSWER:

```
1. def function(x, y):
2.     return x ** y + 100
```

Exercises

PROBLEM: Which function definitions are valid?

```
1.  @foo(bar):

2.  _foo(bar = 1):

3.  foo(bar = 2, bla = 1):

4.  foo(bar = 2, bla):

5.  foo($bar, bla = 1):
```

ANSWER:

```
1.  invalid: symbol  @  in function's name
2.  valid
3.  valid: there are several arguments with default values
4.  invalid: argument without default value
5.  invalid: symbol  $  in argument's name
```

Exercises

PROBLEM: Change the function below to return the greeting instead of printing it:

```
1.  def hi():
2.      greeting = "Hello world!!!"
3.      print(greeting)
```

YOUR CODE:

```
1
2
3
4
5
6
```

ANSWER:

```
1.  def hi():
2.      greeting = "Hello world!!!"
3.      return greeting
```

If/Else and conditional statements

There are a lot of uses for the simple statements and operations we have covered so far in this book. However, the main purpose of any programming is to implement some kind of logic.

If/else blocks are a core syntax element in Python. They let you conditionally control the flow of the program.

In the following scenario, you want to know if your car is travelling too quickly. If you are exceeding 100 km/h, the function will print "Too fast!" If you drive below the speed limit, the function will print "You are driving below the speed limit. Well done."

This is what that code would look like.:

```
1.  def drive(car_speed):
2.
3.      if car_speed > 100:
4.          print("Too fast!")
5.      else:
6.          print("You are driving below the speed limit. Well done")
```

```
>>> drive(70)
You are driving below the speed limit. Well done
>>> drive(120)
Too fast!
```

There are multiple things to note in the code above.

First, the > operator. It's a Boolean comparison operator, the same as the one used in maths. It returns *True* if the first item is larger than the second, and *False* otherwise.

Second, the *if/else* syntax. If *is_too_fast* is *True*, the first block of code is executed. If not, the second block of code is executed.

Third, the indentation. The statements inside the function are indented, and then the statements inside the *if/else* block are further indented.

47

Boolean expressions

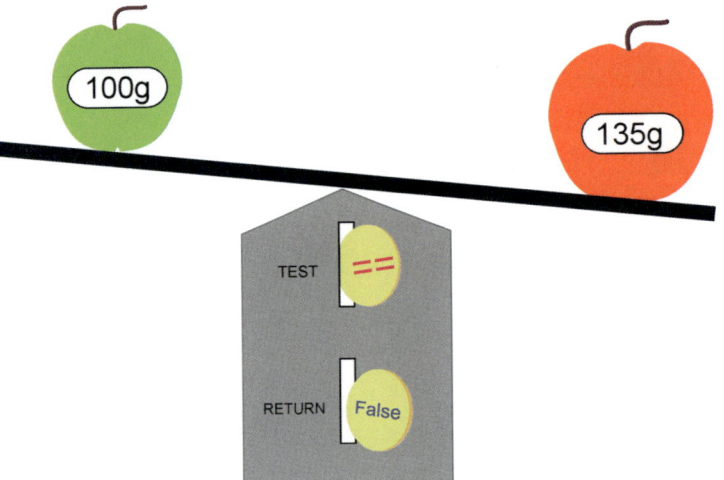

```
greenApple = 100
redApple = 135

print(greenApple == redApple)        #test if 100 and 135 are equal
#False

print(greenApple < redApple)         #test if 100 is less than 135
#True

print(greenApple != redApple)        #test if not equal
#True
```

```
>>> bool(1)
True
>>> bool("")
False
>>> bool(None)
False
>>> bool("blah")
True
>>> bool(0)
False
>>> bool(True)
True
```

In Python any value can be interpreted as True or False. Among the data types values 0, "" - an empty string, None and False itself are False. Any other value is True.

You may check if the value is True or False by converting the value to a boolean type:

Also there are several built-in comparison operators like > return True or False when called. The table below provides an overview of these operators.

Operator	Statement	Statement's return value
Less	`1 < 2`	True
	`4 < 3`	False
Less or equal	`2 <= 2`	True
	`4 <= 3`	False
Greater	`2 > 1`	True
	`3 > 3`	False
Greater or equal	`2 >= 2`	True
	`3 >= 4`	False
Equal	`"foo" == "foo"`	True
	`0 == 1`	False
Not equal	`"foo" != "bar"`	True
	`11 != (10 + 1)`	False
And (both parts must be True)	`3 and "foo"`	True
	`None and True`	False
Or (one of parts must be True)	`1 or None`	True
	`None or False`	False
Not (opposite to the target expression)	`not None`	True
	`not True`	False

Note, comparison operators have higher precedence than the logical operators "and", "or" and "not". All maths operators have higher precedence than comparison operators. Here are several compound examples to illustrate how to use boolean operators:

```
>>> 2 * 6 + 1 < 2 * (6 + 1)
True
>>> 2 * 6 + 1 == 2 * (6 + 1) - 1
True
>>> 2 ** 3 == 8 and 2 ** 2 == 16
False
>>> (2 ** 2 == 4 and False) or (not (16 < 15 or 1 == 3))
True
```

49

Alternative branches

In many cases the logic can be more sophisticated than just two conditions.

Let's modify the speed function we created before to respond to speeds over 200 km/h by printing "You are insane, man!!!" and printing "The optimal speed for your car." when the speed is between 70 and 80 km/h.

```python
1.  def drive(car_speed):
2.      if car_speed > 200:
3.          print("You are insane, man!!!")
4.      elif car_speed > 100:
5.          print("Too fast!")
6.      elif car_speed > 70 and car_speed < 80:
7.          print("The optimal speed for your car.")
8.      else:
9.          print("You are driving below the speed limit. Well done")
```

You might notice that in the code above we don't use a separate Boolean variable. Instead, we place the comparison operator inline with the if statement. The "and" statement links two comparison operators together.

We also use the keyword "elif". This defines an alternate branch. Be careful with the order of branches! If more than one branch is True, only the first one will be used. For example:

```python
1.  a = 10
2.
3.  if a > 1:
4.      print("Big")
5.  elif a > 5:
6.      print("Really big")
7.  elif a == 10:
8.      print("Approaching enormity")
9.  elif a > 10:
10.     print("Enormous!")
```

This code will only ever print "Big", and the other statements will be ignored.

50

Quiz

Try to answer these questions without using the interpreter.

1. What are the boolean values - bool(a) - for the following variables:

```
1.  a = False
2.  a = "0"
3.  a = 0 * 18
4.  a = "None"
```

2. What is the output of the following statement:
   (2 ** 2 == 4 and False) or (not (16 > 15 or 1 == 3))

3. Name Python's logical operators

4. What will be printed as a result of the following code?

```
1.  x = 5
2.  if x == 25:
3.      print ("Quarter")
4.  elif x == 10:
5.      print ("Dime")
6.  elif x == 5
7.      print ("Nickel")
8.  elif x == 1:
9.      print ("Penny")
10. else:
11.     print ("Not a coin")
```

5. Suppose x=5, y=0, and z=1. Are the following expressions True or False?

```
1.  x == 0
2.  x >= y
3.  2 + 3 == x and y < 1
4.  not (z == 0 or y == 0)
5.  x = 3
```

51

Quiz

6. What does the following code print?

```
1.  x = 0
2.  if x != 0:
3.      print("x is nonzero")
```

ANSWER:

1. a) False

   b) True - this is a string with a character 0 not an integer

   c) False - 0 * 18 is 0

   d) True - again "None" is a string not the actual None

2. False - the expression inside the "not" statement is True, making that statement False, and the first statement is also False.

3. and, or, not

4. Nickel. x == 25 and x == 10 are False, so the first True statement is x == 5.

5. a) False. The operator == tests for equality, and 5 does not equal 0.

   b) True. 5 is greater than or equal to 0.

   c) True. Both 2 + 3 == x and y < 1 are True.

   d) False. y == 0 is True, so z == 0 or y == 0 is True, and its negation is False.

   c) True. The = operator assigns the value 3 to x, and the value 3 evaluates to True.

6. Nothing. The expression is False, so the code is not executed.

Exercises

PROBLEM: Write an expression that tests if a variable *x* is less than or equal to 100.

YOUR CODE:

```
1
2
3
4
5
6
```

ANSWER:

```
1.  x <= 100
```

Exercises

PROBLEM: Write an expression that tests if a variable **x** is between 3 and 10, inclusive.

YOUR CODE:

```
1
2
3
4
5
6
```

ANSWER:

```
1.  x >= 3 and x <= 10
```

Exercises

PROBLEM: Write an expression that tests if a variable **x** is even or a multiple of 5.

YOUR CODE:

```
1
2
3
4
5
6
```

ANSWER:

```
1.  (x % 2 == 0) or (x % 5 == 0)
```

Exercises

PROBLEM:
There is a function with the following declaration: *person_is_old(age)* which returns *True* or *False* based on the incoming age as an integer.
Write a function that uses the one mentioned above so that it prints "Go to work!" if the person is not old and "You deserved to have a long vacation" otherwise. Your function must also accept the age as its argument.

YOUR CODE:

```
1
2
3
4
5
6
```

ANSWER:

```python
def tell_what_to_do(age):
    if person_is_old(age):
        print("You deserved to have a long vacation")
    else:
        print("Go to work!")
```

Classes and objects

One of the key principles of object-oriented programming is encapsulation - hiding the details of the inner workings of the system, so that the user doesn't need to know how it works in order to use it. The part of the program that the user interacts with is called the "interface".

Just as the driver of a car needs tools like a steering wheel and a gas pedal to use the car's capabilities, users of your code need to use syntax constructs called methods.

Here, we have implemented a car in Python:

```python
1.   class Car:
2.
3.       def turn_left(self):
4.           pass
5.
6.       def turn_right(self):
7.           pass
8.
9.       def accelerate(self):
10.          pass
11.
12.      def slow_down(self):
13.          pass
14.
15.      def open_a_window(self):
16.          pass
```

In the code above, we have created a class. A class is an entity that has specific behaviours. These behaviours take the form of methods, which are the same as the functions we have used previously, and are indented in the same way. The methods of a class are given the class ("self") as their first parameter. The "pass" keyword tells Python that this code block does nothing.

There are a variety of different cars that this class could represent - BMW, Mercedes, Audi, Fiat, Tesla, and many others. Let's create a car with some parameters.

```python
1.   bmw_x6 = Car(model = "BMW X6", max_speed = 230)
```

57

Classes and objects

In the code above you can see that the car object was created with two parameters: model and max_speed. The original car code has nothing that would support them. In order to implement this support you must introduce an _init_ method:

```
1.  class Car:
2.
3.      def __init__(self, model, max_speed):
4.          self.model = model
5.          self.max_speed = max_speed
6.          self.speed = 0
7.
8.          ...
```

The code above takes your new car object ("self") and uses the dot notation to assign the car's model and max_speed. The car begins with a speed of zero.

The _init_ method shouldn't contain a return statement - it's just used to build your object. This method is called the "class constructor".

Accelerating and slowing down should decrease and increase the car's speed appropriately:

```
1.  class Car:
2.
3.          ...
4.      def accelerate(self, speed_difference):
5.          self.speed += abs(speed_difference)
6.          self.speed = min(self.speed, self.max_speed)
7.
8.      def slow_down(self, speed_difference):
9.          self.speed -= abs(speed_difference)
10.         self.speed = max(self.speed, -5)
11.
12.         ....
```

The internal state of the object is changed using the dot notation.

The min and max functions are used to guarantee that the car never exceeds the maximum speed, or travels below -5 km/h (reverse transmission)

The following code would accelerate the car by 30 km/h.

```
1.  bmw_x6.accelerate(30)
```

When you're creating more than one class, you may want some of them to have relationship with each other. For example, a Car is a Vehicle, and a Bus is also a Vehicle. Although they share many similarities, they have very different internal structures.

To reflect similarities and differences in objects, Python has a feature called inheritance.

In this example, we implement a Vehicle class, which has model and max_speed parameters like the Car class.

```
1.  class Vehicle:
2.
3.      def __init__(self, model, max_speed):
4.          self.model = model
5.          self.max_speed = max_speed
6.          self.speed = 0
7.
8.      def accelerate(self, speed_difference):
9.          self.speed += abs(speed_difference)
10.         self.speed = min(self.speed, self.max_speed)
11.
12.     def slow_down(self, speed_difference):
13.         self.speed -= abs(speed_difference)
14.         self.speed = max(self.speed, -5)
15.
16.         ...
```

Classes and objects

Now we want to create Car and Bus classes; the Car class is identical, but the Bus class doesn't have a reverse transmission.

```python
1.  class Car(Vehicle):
2.      pass
3.
4.  class Bus(Vehicle):
5.
6.      def slow_down(self, speed_difference):
7.          super().slow_down(speed_difference)
8.          self.speed = max(self.speed, 0)
```

The word "Vehicle" between the perentheses after the class name makes the Car and Bus classes inherit from Vehicle.

In the Bus class, the slow_down method overrides the behavior of the parent class.
The super() statement makes a call to the parent class to find the new speed, and then makes sure that this speed is not below 0 km/h.

Quiz

PROBLEM:

1. What would a software engineer call a collection of behaviors that the user can use?

2. What is the name of the relationship between classes?

3. What is the general term for methods used to create objects in Python? For example, the following method: _init_(name, max_speed).

4. What is missing from the method in the previous question?

ANSWER:

1. Interface

2. Inheritance

3. class constructor.

4. self argument is missing

Exercises

PROBLEM: Write Python code that would make BMW X6 accelerate by 100 km/h

YOUR CODE:

```
1
2
3
4
5
6
```

ANSWER:

```
1.  bmw_x6.accelerate(100)
```

Exercises

PROBLEM: Introduce a Bike class that is also a Vehicle. The main feature of a bike is that it can never ever be faster than 30 km/h.

YOUR CODE:

```
1
2
3
4
5
6
```

ANSWER: You just need to make sure that max speed is capped by 30 km/h in Bike's constructor

```python
1.  class Bike(Vehicle):
2.
3.      def __init__(self, name, max_speed):
4.          max_speed = min(max_speed, 30)
5.          super().__init__(name, max_speed)
```

Exercises

PROBLEM:
Add to your code from the previous exercise a new method called *show_status* that prints something like *"The bike is BMX, its speed is 27 km/h"*

YOUR CODE:
```
1
2
3
4
5
6
```

ANSWER:
Method's implementation is supposed to look the following way:

```
1.  def show_status(self):
2.      print("The bike is " + self.name + ", its speed is " +
        str(self.speed) + " km/h")
```

In many cases, you want to perform the same action on a lot of very similar objects. For example, in real life, you might want to iron your socks. It wouldn't make sense for you to consider each one individually as a unique object requiring special treatment.

In programming, this is where Python collections come in handy. A good analogy for collections is a set of lockers.

Python has two types of lockers: ones with name tags, and anonymous ones, indexed only by number.

To access items in the anonymous locker room, you can either go through all the lockers one by one, or access a specific one by an integer index. In Python, these lockers are represented by lists and tuples.

For lockers with name tags, you can either go through each locker one by one, or you can look at a specific name tag. In Python, these lockers are represented by dictionaries.

This chapter provides an overview of built-in Python collections.

Lists and tuples use integers for indexing.   Dictionaries use keys for indexing.

65

Tuples

Tuples are immutable arrays of variables.

my_tuple = ("apple" , "pear" , "banana")

You can access the elements of tuples in the following way:

```
>>> my_tuple = ("apple", "pear", "banana")
>>> my_tuple[1:]              # from second to the end
'pear', 'banana'
>>> my_tuple[2][2]            # 3rd character of 3rd item
'n'
```

"Immutable" means that once you define a tuple, you can't change it.

```
>>> my_tuple[2] = "mango"              # replace 'banana' with 'mango'
TypeError: 'tuple' object does not support item assignment
['apple', 'pear', 'mango']
>>> my_tuple[2][0] = "B"               # try to change the 'b' with "B" and you
                                       # will get an error
TypeError: 'str' object does not support item assignment
```

```
>>> new_tuple = ('foo', 'bar', 'zoo', 'loo')
>>> type(new_tuple)
<class 'tuple'>
>>> new_tuple[0]
'foo'
>>> new_tuple[3]
'loo'
>>> new_tuple[1:3]
('bar', 'zoo')
>>> len(new_tuple)
4
>>> new_tuple * 2
('foo', 'bar', 'zoo', 'loo', 'foo', 'bar', 'zoo', 'loo')
>>> new_tuple + ('blah', 'blah')
('foo', 'bar', 'zoo', 'loo', 'blah', 'blah')
```

You can see from the code snippet above that tuples behave similarly to Python strings - however, strings are arrays of just characters, whereas tuples can contain any kind of variable.

You can slice, index, concatenate, and multiply tuples in the same way that you can with strings.

Syntactically, tuple items must be surrounded by parentheses, and separated by commas. Even tuples containing a single item must have a comma: (1,) is a tuple, but (1) is not.

Lists

Lists are like tuples that you can change after you've created them.

Lets define a simple list with three items:

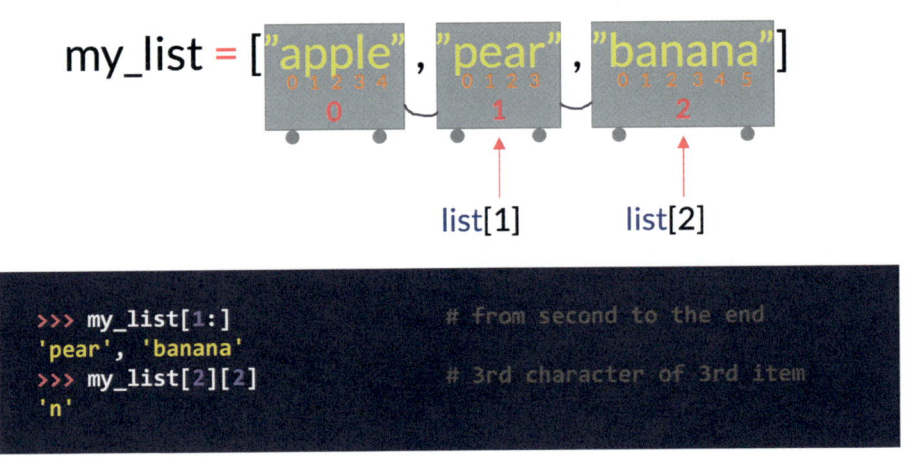

```
>>> my_list[1:]              # from second to the end
'pear', 'banana'
>>> my_list[2][2]            # 3rd character of 3rd item
'n'
```

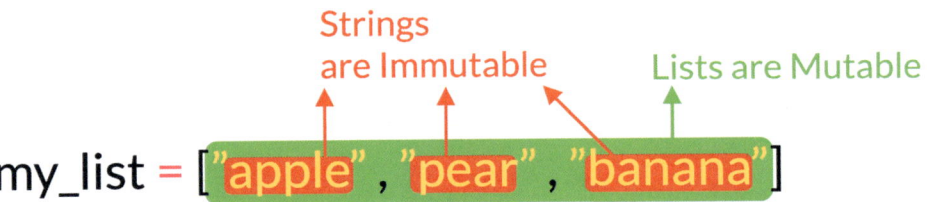

```
>>> my_list[2] = "mango"            #replace 'banana' with 'mango'
>>> my_list
['apple', 'pear', 'mango']
>>> my_list[2][0] = "B"             #try to change the 'b' with "B" and you
                                    #will get an error
TypeError: 'str' object does not support item assignment
```

```
>>> new_list = ['foo', 'bar', 'zoo', 'loo']
```

As you may have noticed, list items are supposed to be enclosed by square brackets.

Now lets remove the 3rd item and change the first one to "blah":

```
>>> new_list.pop(2)
>>> new_list[0] = "blah"
>>> new_list
['blah', 'bar', 'loo']
```

You can add items to the end of the list:

```
>>> new_list.append("new_item")
```

And pop the items from the end of the list:

```
>>> new_list.pop()
'new_item'
```

You can also add the item to a specific position in the list:

```
>>> new_list = ['foo', 'bar', 'zoo', 'loo']
>>> new_list.insert(1, 'John')
>>> new_list
['foo', 'John', 'bar', 'zoo', 'loo']
```

When you add an item to a list, it takes the location you specify and shifts all the following items to the right.

Dictionaries

A dictionary is a collection of keys and values, which works much the same as a list or a tuple. Instead of an integer index, dictionary values can be addressed by indices of almost any type.

Lets create a dictionary with people names as keys and their ages as values:

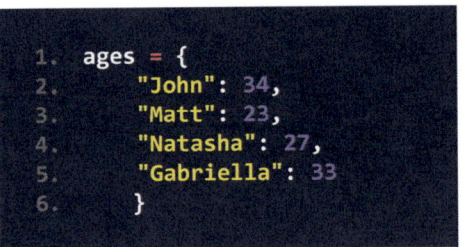

```
1.  ages = {
2.      "John": 34,
3.      "Matt": 23,
4.      "Natasha": 27,
5.      "Gabriella": 33
6.  }
```

The key-value pairs must be enclosed in curly brackets and separated by commas. Keys and values must be separated by a colon.

The keys in the dictionary must be unique, but the values can be the same. A key can be almost any type of variable.

The following is also a valid dictionary:

```
1.   class SomeClass:
2.       pass
3.
4.   obj1 = SomeClass()
5.   obj2 = SomeClass()
6.
7.   a_dict = {
8.       obj1: 11,
9.       obj2: 23
10.      }
```

You may fetch John's age the following way:

```
1.   johns_age = ages["John"]
```

In the same way, you can set the value of elements by key:

```
1.   ages["John"] = 999
```

The above statement either changes the value of an existing key or creates a new key-value pair if none exists.

You can also remove a key-value pair from the dictionary.

```
1.   ages.pop("John")
```

Quiz

PROBLEM:

1. Which collection resembles a locker room with name tags on the lockers? Which one resembles an anonymous locker?

2. What is the main difference between lists and tuples?

3. Can a float be used as a key in a dictionary?

4. How many keys called "John" can you have in a dictionary?

5. Is this a tuple: (123)?

ANSWER:

1. dictionary/list and tuple

2. lists can be modified, tuples can't

3. yes, why not?

4. exactly one - all keys must be unique

5. no - a comma was forgotten

Exercises

PROBLEM: Using Python get Natasha's age.

YOUR CODE:

```
1
2
3
4
5
6
```

ANSWER:

```
1.  ages['Natasha']
```

Exercises

PROBLEM: Get rid of Matt.

YOUR CODE:

```
1
2
3
4
5
6
```

ANSWER:

```
1.  ages.pop('Matt')
```

Collections can be used to store data in, but you can also go through them and do something to each item individually.

In Python there are two types of loop that you can use: while and for.

A while loop carries on repeating as long as a certain condition is true.

The statements inside a while loop must be indented, like any other code block.
The loop must be defined using the *"while"* keyword, a Boolean statement, and a colon.

The Boolean statement could be a function call, a variable, or a comparison statement.

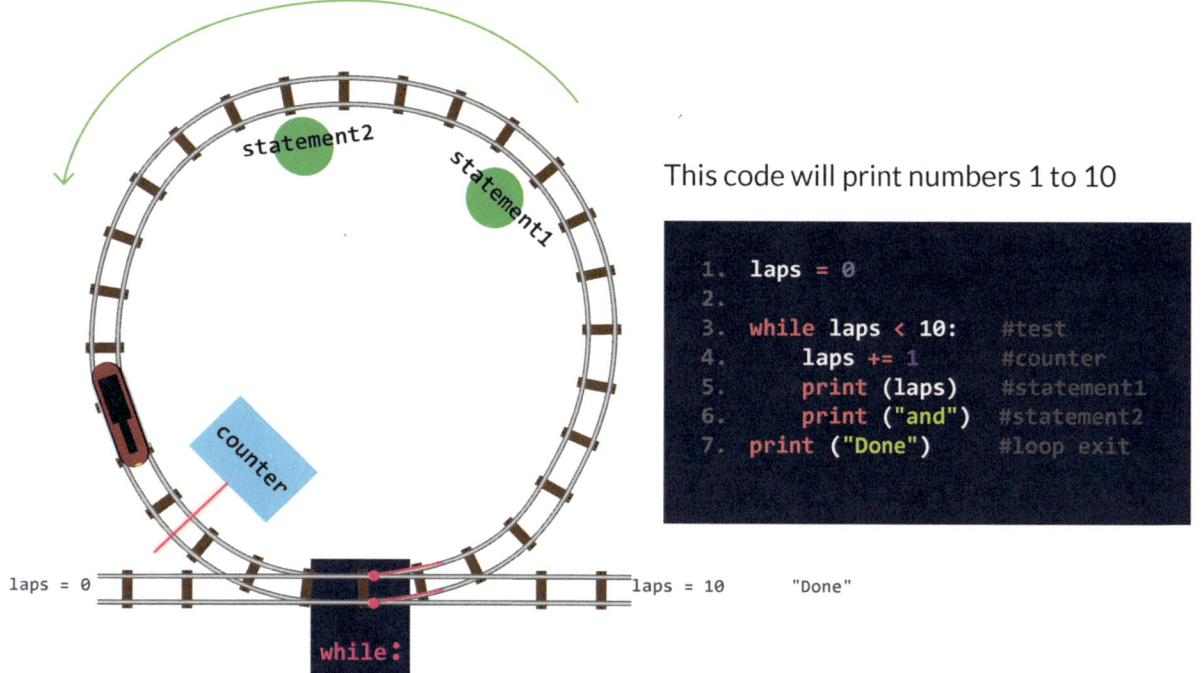

This code will print numbers 1 to 10

```
1.  laps = 0
2.
3.  while laps < 10:      #test
4.      laps += 1         #counter
5.      print (laps)      #statement1
6.      print ("and")     #statement2
7.  print ("Done")        #loop exit
```

75

While

Python provides break and continue statements to have even better control on your loop.

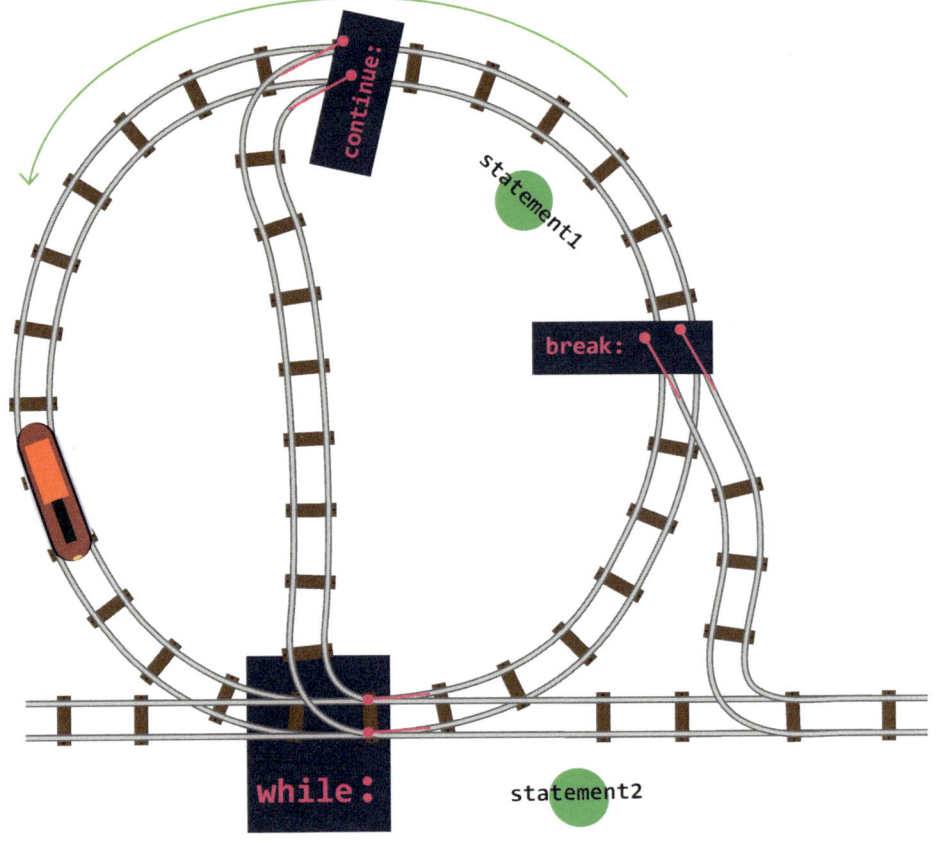

```
1.  while <test1>:
2.      <statement1>
3.      if <test2>: break          #loop exit, skip else
4.      if <test3>: continue       #go to the top <test1>
5.  else:
6.      <statement2>               #run if break didn't happen
```

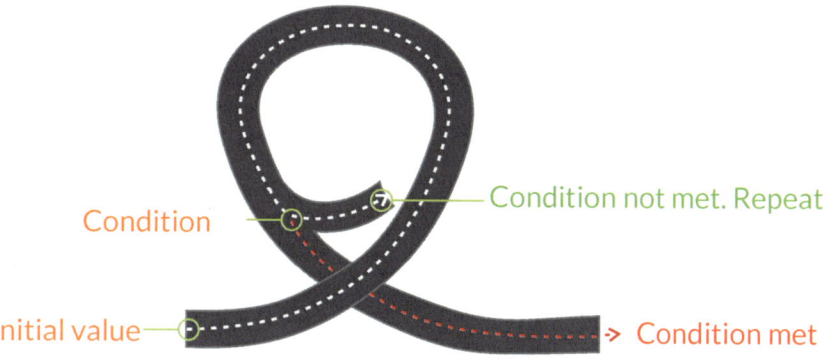

Condition

Condition not met. Repeat

Initial value

Condition met

You can use a "for" loop to iterate though a collection.
Let's say you have the following list:

```
1.  a = ["one", "two", "three"]
```

To print each string individually, you could use this loop:

```
1.  for item in a:
2.      print(item)
```

The loop must be defined using the "for" keyword, the name of the new variable to hold each individual item, the "in" keyword, the name of the collection, and a colon. The statements inside a "for" loop must also be indented.

You can escape from a loop using the "break" command:

```
1.  numbers = [1, 2, 5, 6, 7, 8, 9]
2.
3.  for number in numbers:
4.      print("Looking at: " + str(number))
5.      if number > 6:
6.          print("Too big: " + str(number) + "!")
7.          break
```

Loops

The above code gives the following output:

```
Looking at: 1
Looking at: 2
Looking at: 5
Looking at: 6
Looking at: 7
Too big: 7!
```

The iteration stops after number 7, meaning that numbers 8 and 9 are not included.

You can also skip particular items in a collection using the "continue" keyword:

```
1.  numbers = [1, 6, 7, 8, 9, 2, 5]
2.
3.  for number in numbers:
4.      if number > 6:
5.          continue
6.      print("Looking at: " + str(number))
```

The above code gives the following output:

```
Looking at: 1
Looking at: 6
Looking at: 2
Looking at: 5
```

Here, we ignored numbers 7, 8, and 9.
Dictionaries can be iterated through in the same way.

```
1.  ages = {
2.      "John": 34,
3.      "Matt": 23,
4.      "Natasha": 27,
5.      "Gabriella": 33
6.      }
7.
8.  for name in ages:
9.      print(name)
```

Quiz

PROBLEM:

1. If you wanted to write code that triggered an alarm every ten minutes, as long as you were sleeping, should you use a "for" or a "while" loop?

2. How do you completely stop a while loop? Give two options.

3. How do you skip a specific item in a for loop? Give two options.

ANSWER:

1. while

2. Change while loop's condition to evaluate to False or use a break keyword.

3. Isolate the code for item processing within an if statement or use a continue keyword.

Exercises

PROBLEM:

Write some code to print out the name of the oldest person inside the ages dictionary. This will use knowledge from earlier chapters in the book.

YOUR CODE:

```
1
2
3
4
5
6
```

ANSWER:

```python
1.  ages = {
2.      "John": 34,
3.      "Matt": 23,
4.      "Natasha": 27,
5.      "Gabriella": 33
6.      }
7.
8.  oldest_person = None
9.  current_biggest_age = 0
10.
11. for name in ages:
12.     age = ages[name]
13.     if age > current_biggest_age:
14.         oldest_person = name
15.         current_biggest_age = age
16.
17. print(oldest_person)
```

Most file operations boil down to: opening files, reading files, writing data into files, and closing files. Usually the data you write into a file will be textual.

Let's say you want to write a list of integers into a file so that every integer is on a separate line. First, open the file:

```
1.  the_file = open("integers.txt", "w")
```

The first argument to the "open" function is the path to the file, and the second argument tells Python that you want to write data into the file. This means that the file doesn't have to exist before you begin.

The function returns a file object that you can use later on.

First let's define an array of integers and write them to the file as strings.

```
1.  integers = [1, 2, 3, 4, 5]
2.
3.  for integer in integers:
4.      the_file.write(str(integer) + '\n')
```

The "write" method takes in a string as an argument and writes it to the file.

Note the "\n" symbol - this is the newline character. It starts a new line in the file.

When you're finished with the file, you have to close it:

```
1.  the_file.close()
```

81

File operations

You can also read data from a file.

First, open the file without using the "w" flag:

```
1.  the_file = open("integers.txt")
```

Get all the lines from the file:

```
1.  lines = the_file.readlines()
```

The readlines() functions returns all of the lines in the file as a list of strings.

Let's print out the lines:

```
1.  for line in lines:
2.      print(line)
```

After you execute the code above you shall see the following on the screen:

```
1
2
3
4
5
```

And as with writing to a file - close it when you are done:

```
1.  the_file.close()
```

Quiz

PROBLEM:

1. What does a newline character look like?

2. What are you supposed to do with the file once you are done working with it?

3. Which method is used to put data into the file?

4. What method should you use to get all the lines from the file?

ANSWER:

1. \n

2. Close it

3. write

4. readlines

Exceptions

Sometimes something unexpected happens that stops a program from executing as it should. These events are called "exceptions".

```
>>> 1 / 0
```

After you hit enter, you'll see the following output:

```
Traceback (most recent call last):
    File "<stdin>", line 1, in <module>
ZeroDivisionError: division by zero
```

This is called an exception traceback. It shows you which functions or methods were called before the exception happened. The last line tells you which exception was raised and gives you some additional, human-readable information.
In Python you can achieve this via a *try/except* block.

What if an exception happens in the middle of something important?

Lets print *"division by zero. But it is totally fine."* instead of throwing a traceback.

```
1.  try:
2.      1 / 0
3.  except ZeroDivisionError as e:
4.      print(str(e) + ". But it is totally fine.")
```

In the code above you can see that the statements you want to make an attempt to execute go into the try block. And all the error handling code goes under *except*.

except keyword must be accompanied with a class of the exception. It also can be followed by an as keyword and a variable which is supposed to store a human readable description of the error.

You can define your own exception classes to further on notify that something extraordinary happend inside your code:

```
1.  class YourException(Exception):
2.      pass
```

All custom exceptions must have a built-in Python exception as a superclass. The exceptions do not have to implement any other logic.

In order to throw an exception you should use the *raise* keyword:

```
1.  raise YourException("Human-readable message")
```

Once you execute the code above, you shall see a traceback with "Human-readable message" string as an extra detail.

Handling custom exceptions is not different from handling the built-in ones:

```
1.  try:
2.      raise YourException("Human-readable message")
3.  except YourException as e:
4.      print("Your exception just occured with a message: " + str(e))
```

Quiz

PROBLEM:

1. Which block is supposed to be used to handle exceptions?

2. What is the name of the long text blob that is printed once an exception takes place?

ANSWER:

1. try/except block

2. traceback

Part II: Standard Library

Import statement and Python modules and packages

All source code in Python, as you may have noticed, is stored in various files called modules. Each module has a .py extension. Different modules are logically combined together into collections called packages. A package is a plain folder with _init_.py file.
E.g. the following is a package:

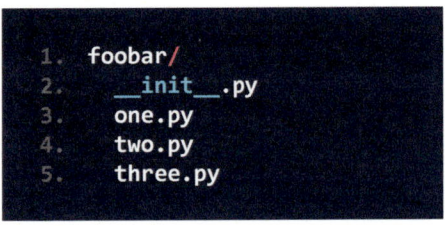

And this one is not:

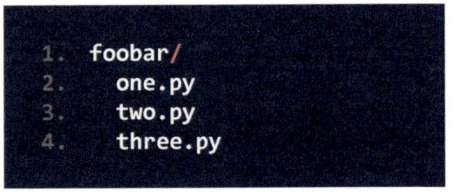

Default Python installation comes with a significant amount of packages.
This set of packages is called a standard library.

If you want to use functionality stored in another package you must use an import statement.

Lets print your user name on the screen using Python interpreter:

```
>>> import getpass
>>> getpass.getuser()
'gunther'
```

The snippet above shows how to import the most top level package. As you can see members of the package are supposed to be accessed via the *dot* operator.

You may avoid using the dot operator by importing the thing you need directly:

```
>>> from getpass import getuser
>>> getuser()
'gunther'
```

To indicate the source of the import you must use from keyword.

Sometimes you may want to use multiple entities from the same package. In this case it is simpler to import all the entities straight away:

```
>>> from sys import pydebug, flags
```

Note, the entities kept inside Python packages can be virtually any Python constructs. A class, a function, a variable, a module or even a package (nested packages are possible).

89

Quiz

PROBLEM:

1. What is the synonym of Python source file?

2. What is the term for folders with Python modules?

3. What is the name of a collection of Packages that comes together with default Python installation?

4. How to import module path from os package?

ANSWER:

1. module

2. package

3. standard library

4. from os import path

File operations using os module

Even though it is possible to work with files using builtin Python functions and methods they do not cover all the scenarios that you may face when manipulating computer file system.

This chapter provides an overview of all the common tasks you may face on the lower level when processing the data and Python means of managing with these tasks.

A quick note: some of the examples below use Linux's path structure. To play with them on Windows replace a slash (/) with a backslash (\).

To begin with lets say you have got the following folder structure (e.g. created using a plain file manager):

```
/parent/
    foo/
        one.txt
        two.txt
        three.txt
```

First navigate to the parent directory of foo using a plain terminal command:

```
cd /parent
```

Lets verify that directory's path is what we expect it to be.

To get the absolute path of the current directory you ought to employ abspath function and curdir property of os.path module:

```
>>> from os.path import abspath, curdir
>>> curdir
'.'
>>> abspath(curdir)
'/parent'
```

curdir variable holds a string pointing to the current directory - .. abspath expects any path as its argument and returns the absolute path.

Now remove one.txt and rename two.txt into bar.txt. To do this you will need two functions from the standard library's os module: remove and rename respectively.

File operations using os module

```
>>> from os import remove, rename
>>> remove("foo/one.txt")
>>> rename("foo/two.txt", "foo/bar.txt")
```

As you may have noticed, in order to get rid of the file you must pass its name to the function and in order to rename the file apart from supplying the original name you are also supposed to pass the string that will be assigned as the file's new name.

Note, when supplying the name of the file you must give either a relative or an absolute path to the file. In case of the absolute path everything is plain and simple - it should start with the root of your file system.

The absolute path could look the following way on UNIX and Windows respectively:

```
/Blah/Blah/foo/one.txt
```

```
C:\Blah\Blah\foo\one.txt
```

Relative paths are calculated with your current directory.
Lets say you are in a directory /foo/bar/one and you want to move to /foo/blah/two.
In this case the relative path shall be: ../../two. Two dots represent a parent directory.
And since you need two navigate two levels above - a sequence of ../../ is required.

Due to the fact that different delimiters are used on *nix and Windows the remove/rename code snippet above has a serious flaw. It is not multi-platform.
In order to transform it into one you should use join function from os.path module:

```
>>> from os import remove, rename
>>> from os.path import join
>>> remove(join("foo", "one.txt"))
>>> rename(join("foo", "two.txt"), join("foo", "bar.txt"))
```

You pass all the parts of the path to the join function as strings, and then the operating system-specific path delimiter is used to produce a string.

You can list all the files and folders in a particular directory:

```
>>> from os import listdir
>>> listdir("foo")
["bar.txt", "three.txt"]
```

Now let's try to remove the foo directory.

```
>>> from os import rmdir
>>> rmdir("foo")
Traceback (most recent call last):
  File "<stdin>", line 1, in <module>
OSError: [Errno 39] Directory not empty: 'foo'
```

Oops! We've cause an exception. The directory can't be deleted as long as it contains anything inside.

Quiz

PROBLEM:

1. What major difference between Windows and Linux filesystems make it more difficult to write cross-platform Python programs?

2. What is the value of os.path.curdir?

3. Which string represents the parent of the current directory?

ANSWER:

1. Different path delimiters: / on Unix and \ on Windows

2. .

3. ..

Exercises

PROBLEM: Fix the "rmdir" code from the last example so that it works.

YOUR CODE:

```
1
2
3
4
5
6
```

ANSWER: To do so you just need to get rid of all the files inside first:

```
>>> remove("foo/bar.txt")    # you renamed it
>>> remove("foo/three.txt")
>>> rmdir("foo")
```

Exercises

PROBLEM: Make the following function cross-platform:

```
1. def show_foobar_here(path):
2.     print(path + "/foobar")
```

YOUR CODE:

```
1
2
3
4
5
6
```

ANSWER:

```
1. from os.path import join
2.
3. def show_foobar_here(path):
4.     print(join(path, "foobar"))
```

Exercises

PROBLEM:
Using the isdir function from the os.path module, find the folder inside your current directory.

Iterate through the files and folders, and then throw a custom DirFound exception with the absolute path of the directory as the human-readable description.

YOUR CODE:

```
1
2
3
4
5
6
```

ANSWER:
The following would be a sufficient solution:

```python
1.  from os.path import isdir, curdir, abspath
2.  from os import listdir
3.
4.  class DirFound(Exception):
5.      pass
6.
7.  def detect_dirs():
8.      for item in listdir(curdir):
9.          if isdir(item):
10.             raise DirFound(abspath(item))
```

Regular Expressions

Although you can use the "in" operator to check if a substring is present within a string, it doesn't tell you where the substring is located, nor does it let you match the substring non-precisely.

Take this string:

```
>>> lorem_text = "Lorem ipsum dolor sit amet, consectetur adipiscing elit, sed do
    eiusmod tempor incididunt ut`labore et dolore magna aliqua."
```

You want to find out if this text contains something like "dolor BLA BLA BLA amet" - the words "dolor" and "amet" in that order, with any amount of text in between.

To do this, you can use the re.search method:

```
>>> import re
>>> found = re.search("dolor .*amet", lorem_text)
>>> found
<_sre.SRE_Match object; span=(12, 26), match='dolor sit amet'>
```

The "search" function takes a regular expression pattern as its first argument, and the text to be searched as its second argument.

The regular expression patter is a flexible description of what you're looking for in the text. The format is covered later in this chapter.

Look at the return value of the search function: it's called a MatchObject, and it tells you where the substring was found in the original text.

If the pattern can't be found, then the function returns None:

```
>>> match = re.search("found", lorem_text)
>>> type(match)
<class 'NoneType'>
```

You may get *start* and *end* indices of the substring from the match object:

```
>>> found.start()
12
>>> found.end()
26
```

and access the substring matched by the pattern:

```
>>> found.group()
'dolor sit amet'
>>> lorem_text[12:26]
'dolor sit amet'
```

Note: if multiple occurrences of the patter are found, only the first one is returned. If you need to go through all of the occurrences, use the re.finditer function:

```
>>> list(re.finditer("dolor .*amet", lorem_text))
[<_sre.SRE_Match object; span=(12, 26), match='dolor sit amet'>]
```

If you want to see if a string matches a certain pattern, you should use the re.match function, which tries to apply the pattern to the whole string:

```
>>> bool(re.match("[0-9][a-z]*", "0dgfgfg"))
True
>>> bool(re.match("[0-9][a-z]*", "dgfgfg"))
False
```

The symbols ".*" in the regular expression pattern match to zero or more arbitrary characters. A dot represents an arbitrary character, and a star represents a cardinality. This is the basic structure of any regular expression pattern: a symbol type, followed by its cardinality.

99

Regular Expressions

The table below provides an overview of the most frequently-used cardinalities.

Cardinality	Description
*	Zero or more
+	One or more
?	Zero or one
{m}	Exact number of symbols
{m, n}	At least m and n at most

This is how to easy remember some of them:

Matches the beginning of a line

Also can mean "NOT"

```
>>> import re
>>> print (re.search('^Beginning','Beginning of line'))
>>> print (re.search('[^line]', 'Beginning of line'))        # not line
```

Matches the end of a line

```
>>> import re
>>> print (re.search('end$','Find me at the end'))
```

Regular Expressions

```
import re
txt = "The quick brown fox jumps over the lazy dog quick"
```

| or	```x = re.findall("quick|dog", txt)``` ```['quick', 'dog']```
1+ → **+** one or more	```x = re.findall("quick+", txt)``` ```['quick', 'quick']```
0+ → **0** → ***** zero or more	```x = re.findall("quick*", txt)``` ```['quick', 'quick']```
01 → **1** / **0** → **?** zero or one	```x = re.findall("quick?", txt)``` ```['quick', 'quick']```
( ) group	```x = re.findall("quick ([a-z]+)", txt)``` ```['brown']```
{ } exactly	```x = re.findall("[Tt]he ([a-z]{4})", txt)``` ```['lazy']```
{x,y} at least X and at most Y	```x = re.findall("[Tt]he ([a-z]{4,5})", txt)``` ```['quick', 'lazy']```
. any single character	```x = re.findall("jumps.+dog", txt)``` ```['jumps over the lazy dog']```

Regular Expressions

This table shows the most frequently-used symbols.

Symbol	Description
.	Any character
\"	Double quote character
\'	Single quote character
\\	Backslash
\t	Tab character
\n	New line character
[0-9]	Any digit from 0 to 9 inclusively
[^0-9]	Any character that is not a digit
[a-z]	Any lowercase letter
[^a-z]	Any character that is not a lowercase letter
[a-zA-Z0-9_]	Any digit, any letter or an underscore

As you can see, some symbols start with a backslash. These symbols are called escape sequences and represent things that either can't be described otherwise or are reserved characters.

Now let's try to compose patterns that combine both symbols and cardinalities.

One or more digit: [0-9]+

An optional number that does not start with zero: ([1-9]{1}[0-9]+)?
Parentheses let you combine multiple symbols into symbol groups and apply cardinalities to the whole groups. You may rephrase the regular expression mentioned above the following way: zero or one number that begins with exactly one digit that is not zero and multiple arbitrary digits afterwards.

A string that may contain any lowercase letter but can't be preceded with an underscore [^_] [a-z]*

In order to replace the first occurrence of a substring with another value you ought to use re.sub function. Replace dolor BLA BLA BLA amet with foobar the following way:

```
re.sub("dolor .*amet", "foobar", lorem_text)
```

Quiz

PROBLEM:

1. What is the escape sequence for a new line character?

2. What is the escape sequence for a tab character?

3. What does the *re.search* function return if the pattern could not be found?

4. What is going to be matched by the following call:
   re.search(r'..d', 'food bar')?
   Try to answer without the interpreter.

ANSWERS:

1. \n

2. \t

3. None

4. ood

Exercises

PROBLEM:

Write a function *is_valid_Python_variable_name(string)* that would say if the string can be used as a variable name in Python. You don't need to worry about reserved keywords.

YOUR CODE:

```
1
2
3
4
5
6
```

ANSWER:

```
1.  def is_valid_Python_variable_name(string):
2.      # underscore or a letter followed by an integer,
3.      # underscore or a character
4.      found = re.match("[_A-Za-z][_a-zA-Z0-9]*", string)
5.      return bool(found)
```

Exercises

PROBLEM:

Write a function *get_number_of_occurrences(string, substring)* that would return an integer that calculates how many instances of a substring were found in a string.

YOUR CODE:

```
1
2
3
4
5
6
```

ANSWER:

```python
1.  def get_number_of_occurrences(string, substring):
2.      findings = list(re.finditer(substring, string))
3.      return len(findings)
```

Math module

This chapter provides an overview of the math module from the Python standard library. The module contains implementations of common mathematical operations, such as square root, that aren't inclcuded in the standard function set.

Using the *math* module you can perform regular trigonometric operations:

```
>>> math.sin(math.radians(30))
0.49999999999999994
>>> math.cos(math.radians(60))
0.5000000000000001
>>> math.tan(math.radians(45))
0.9999999999999999
```

Note, the argument is a value of the angle in radians not degrees. This is why an additional call to math.radians was used.

Also, you see 0.4999999999 instead of 0.5 or 0.99999999999 instead of 1.
This is due to the way the language handles floating point number calculations.

You can get special numbers, like pi and e, to a certain level of precision:

```
>>> math.pi
3.141592653589793
>>> math.e
2.718281828459045
```

You can also calculate square roots:

```
>>> math.sqrt(16)
4.0
>>> math.sqrt(25)
5.0
```

Quiz

PROBLEM:

In order to answer the following questions you need to dive into the standard library

1. What function would you use to calculate an arctangent?
2. What function should be used for exponentiation?
3. How would you calculate a factorial of a number?

ANSWERS:

1. math.atan
2. math.exp
3. math.factorial

JSON

In software engineering there is a process called serialization. The main purpose of it is to transform arbitrary object's state into something that could be transfered over the wire and/or stored in such a manner that the original object could be reconstructed later on. The process of reconstruction is called deserialization.

A real life analogy of serialization is the process of investigating an existing artifact (e.g. a car) and making a detailed blueprint of it (engine, wheels, transmission, etc). Sending serialized data over the wire is similar to sending the blueprint over a normal mail. And deserialization is the process of constructing a copy of the original object by someone based on the fetched blueprints.

In the realm of web programming two standards of data serialization gained highest popularity. XML and JSON. Both are textual which implies that data represented using these standards can be easily viewed by a human-being via a simple text editor like VIM. The subject of this chapter is JSON and the means of Python to serialize data using it.

JSON is a native way to operate with data in JavaScript programming language.

As a format JSON operates with three major constructs.

1. Primitives: integers, floating point numbers, strings, booleans and null datatype
2. Objects: equivalents of Python dictionaries
3. Arrays: equivalents of Python lists

As you can see all JSON constructs perfectly match Python built-in types. Thus the main purpose of serialization of Python data structures into JSON is to transform Python built-in types into a JSON string that could be e.g. sent as a payload inside of an HTTP request/response body.

By default Python can serialize the following datatypes: int, bool, None, str, float, long, dict and list. There are ways of extending this functionality but they are out of the scope of this chapter.

Python's module responsible for serialization is called *json*. It contains two major functions: **dumps** and **loads**. **Dumps** expects Python data structure as the input and returns JSON string as the output. **Loads** does the inverse - it expects a JSON string as an input and returns Python data structure as an output.

108

Code Examples

Import JSON module

```
1.  import json
```

Serialize a list of strings into JSON array

```
1.  list_of_strings = ["one", "two", "three", "four"]
2.  json_array = json.dumps(list_of_strings)
```

Deserialize a JSON object into a Python data structure

```
1.  json_data = """
2.      {
3.        "integer": 1,
4.        "inner_object": {
5.          "nothing": null,
6.          "boolean": false,
7.          "string": "foo"
8.        },
9.        "list_of_strings": [
10.          "one",
11.          "two"
12.        ]
13.      }
14.  """
15.
16.  python_dict = json.loads(json_data)
```

Serialize an integer

```
print (json.dumps(1))
1
print (type(json.dumps(1)))
<class 'str'>
```

109

Code Samples

Serialize a string

```
>>> print(json.dumps("FOO"))
"FOO"
>>> print(len(json.dumps("FOO")))
5
```

Try to deserialize something. that is not JSON - ValueError is raised when the input can't be processed

```
>>> json.loads("FOO")
Traceback ...
...
ValueError: No JSON object could be decoded
```

Try to serialize something. that does not have a representation in JSON - only a limited set of Python built-in types is supported by default

```
>>> class Teacher(object):
        pass
>>> t = Teacher()
>>> json.dumps(t)
Traceback ...
...
TypeError: <...Teacher instance at ...> is not JSON serializable
```

Quiz

PROBLEM:

1. Which function is responsible for JSON serialization in Python?

2. What is the antonym of "serialization"? Which Python function is responsible for it?

3. What is the output of this command: print (json.dumps("FOO")[0]) ?

4. What is the output of this command: print (len(json.dumps(None))) ?

5. What is the output of this command: print (type(json.dumps('"1.57"'))) ?

ANSWER:

1. json.dumps

2. deserialization / json.loads

3. "[1]

4. 4

5. <type 'str'>[2]

---

[1] if you answered F - you forgot that JSON representation of a string includes quotation marks as well

[2] if you answered float - you missed double quotes inside JSON string

Exercises

PROBLEM:

There is the following code:
Implement *join_two_arrays* function

```
>>> array_of_strings_one = '["one", "two"]'
>>> array_of_strings_two = '["three", "four"]'
>>> print join_two_arrays(array_of_strings_one, array_of_strings_
    two)
["one", "two", "three", "four"]
>>> type(join_two_arrays(array_of_strings_one, array_of_strings_
    two))
<class 'str'>
```

YOUR CODE:

```
1
2
3
4
5
6
```

ANSWER:

```
1.  def join_two_arrays(array_of_strings_one, array_of_strings_two)
2.      list_one = json.loads(array_of_strings_one)
3.      list_two = json.loads(array_of_strings_two)
4.      joined_list = list_one + list_two
5.      return json.dumps(joined_list)
```

Exercises

PROBLEM:

There is the following code:
Implement *jsonize_if_not_already_json* function.

```
>>> print jsonize_if_not_already_json("ONE")
"ONE"
>>> print jsonize_if_not_already_json('"ONE"')
"ONE"

>>> print jsonize_if_not_already_json(False)
false
>>> print jsonize_if_not_already_json("false")
false

>>> print jsonize_if_not_already_json("1")
1
>>> print jsonize_if_not_already_json(1)
1
```

YOUR CODE:

```
1
2
3
4
5
6
```

ANSWER:

```
1.  def jsonize_if_not_already_json(value):
2.      try:
3.          value = json.loads(value)
4.      except ValueError:
5.          pass
6.      return json.dumps(value)
```

SQL: sqlite3

One of the main principles of software development is reusability. The principle can be rephrased as DRY - Don't Repeat Yourself. The best way to achieve it is to avoid reinventing the wheel and apply the solutions that were implemented before you.

Over the decades of industry development in information processing and data storage, a common set of constraints has emerged. In this context, the word "constraint" means a set of rules that you apply to the data to be stored.

To understand what constraints are think about an email address. The address is expected to have an "@" character. This expectation is a constraint.

A real-life system with multiple constraints is an automobile assembly line. All the parts are expected to fit certain criteria - if they don't, it's not possible to fully automate the line, and you have to involve manual labor. A general rule of thumb is that to achieve a reasonable level of automation, you must sacrifice a fraction of the input's flexibility.

To create a common system of constraints, the existing systems were combined into what is now called a relational database.

Data are stored in the relational database as tables, where each column represents a set of rules for what data types (strings, ints, booleans, etc.) can be stored in each row.

Each column has a type that represents a rule for the database engine regarding what sort of data can be stored in respective fields. The types can be integers, strings, booleans, etc.

The primary key constraint defines which field should be used as the main index, i.e. which piece of information in the row can be used as its address. A word index means exactly the same thing as in post industry. It is a unique identifier used to simplify access to information. In case of post it is the address of a particular recipient, in case of relational database - a particular row in the table.

Another important rule is a *foreign key constraint*.
It facilitates with enforcing referential integrity.

To illustrate the meaning of *referential integrity* it is the best to have a look at the following real life example.

If a student were to leave a school to attend another school, their name must be removed from the register in all of their classes. Similarly, if you want to remove an item from a relational database, you must also remove all references to it in the database.

The process of removing students from respective courses whenever they change school in the context of relational database is called *referential integrity management*. Foreign key constraints tell you which columns contain references to other places in the database.

There are dozens of other constraints. And even though they won't be covered in this chapter the ones that were already briefly introduced are enough to get a reasonable understanding about how relational databases behave.

The last thing you need to know about before we move on is Structured Query Language (SQL). SQL is a programming language specifically used for declaring database constraints, and for manipulating data (i.e. listing, viewing, creating, updating, or deleting data).

Python sqlite3

Python has a built-in database module called sqlite3.
It is a full stack Python implementation of a relational database and SQL.

Here we will briefly go through major SQL statements and database constructs.

To begin with, open your Python interpreter and import sqlite3

```
1.  import sqlite3
```

Initialize database connection:

```
1.  conn = sqlite3.connect('example.db')
```

Get a cursor:

```
1.  cursor = conn.cursor()
2.  cursor.execute("PRAGMA foreign_keys = ON")
```

Cursor is just a Python object used to execute SQL statements. In sqlite3 foreign key constraints are disabled by default for performance reasons. *PRAGMA* statement enables them.

Now let's create a simple *users* table.

```
1.  cursor.execute("""
2.      CREATE TABLE users(
3.          id INTEGER NOT NULL PRIMARY KEY AUTOINCREMENT,
4.          email TEXT NOT NULL,
5.          name TEXT NOT NULL
6.      )
7.  """)
```

In the code above you may see the following:

> every user must have an email and a name that are text values

> every user has an integer identifier that is used as a primary key. *AUTOINCREMENT* means that whenever new user is created *id* shall be generated automatically based on the identifier of a user stored previously

Also lets create a table called *cars* in such a way that every car mentioned in the table shall have exactly one owner from the list of humans listed in the *users* table.

```
1.   cursor.execute("""
2.       CREATE TABLE cars(
3.           id INTEGER NOT NULL PRIMARY KEY AUTOINCREMENT,
4.           brand TEXT NOT NULL,
5.           model TEXT NOT NULL,
6.           owner INTEGER NOT NULL,
7.           FOREIGN KEY(owner) REFERENCES users(id) ON DELETE CASCADE
8.       )
9.   """)
```

In the code above there is a foreign key definition that denotes a relationship between cars and users in a form of ownership. The *ON DELETE CASCADE* statement tells the database that whenever a user is removed all the cars that belong to the users must be removed as well.

Lets create one user and two cars that belongs to this user:

```
1.   cursor.execute('INSERT INTO users VALUES(NULL, '
2.                   '"john.smith@pythonvisually.com", "John Smith")')
3.   cursor.execute('INSERT INTO cars VALUES(NULL, "Fiat", "Polo", 1)')
4.   cursor.execute('INSERT INTO cars VALUES(NULL, "BMW", "X6", 1)')
```

117

Note, when creating cars we passed value *1* for the owner. We knew that user *John Smith* was the first one created in the database. Thus, his *ID* would logically be *1*

Let's attempt to create a car that references a user who does not exist, e.g. user #2.

```
cursor.execute('INSERT INTO cars VALUES(NULL, "Mazda", "6", 2)')
```

You are expected to see a traceback with the following error message:

```
sqlite3.IntegrityError: FOREIGN KEY constraint failed
```

This way database engine notifies you that something is wrong with the a foreign key you try to store.

Now, let's manipulate the test data that we've created.
First, let's change John's email:

```
cursor.execute('UPDATE users SET email="john.smith@pythonvisually.com"'
               'WHERE name="John Smith"')
```

The above code uses the UPDATE command and the WHERE statement. In combination, they let you update all the values that fit your search criteria.

Now, let's check that the email actually got updated:

```
rows = list(cursor.execute(
    'SELECT email FROM users WHERE name="John Smith"'))
[("john.smith@pythonvisually.com",)]
```

118

When choosing which user to check we used SELECT command. During selection we stated that we are interested only in user's email. In case of row selection cursor's execute method returned and iterator over database rows that we transformed into a list and printed.

Lets get rid of one of the cars, e.g. BMW:

```
1.  cursor.execute('DELETE FROM cars WHERE brand="BMW"')
2.  rows = list(cursor.execute('SELECT * FROM cars'))
3.  len(rows) == 1
```

To remove the row we used DELETE command. After that we verified that total amount of cars was one.

And last but not least, lets check how ON DELETE CASCADE statement works. Lets get rid of Mr. John.

```
cursor.execute('DELETE FROM users WHERE name="John Smith"')
```

Now check how many cars we have left in the database:

```
1.  rows = list(cursor.execute('SELECT * FROM cars'))
2.  print len(rows)
3.  len(rows) == 0
```

This is it. *Fiat* was removed from the database together with its owner.

119

Quiz

PROBLEM:

1. What does the acronym 'SQL' stand for?
2. What sort of integrity do foreign keys help to enforce?
3. How many different fields with the same value can exist in a primary key column?
4. SQL is used for two purposes. Name them.
5. If you want to change an existing row which command should you use?
6. In what form is data stored inside relational databases?
7. Constraints are usually applied to which part of a database?
8. Which entities do individual records in the database represent?
9. What does the acronym 'DRY' stand for?

ANSWER:

1. Structured Query Language
2. Referential integrity
3. Exactly one. Each primary key value must be unique
4. Data definition and data manipulation
5. UPDATE
6. In the form of tables
7. To an individual column
8. Rows
9. Don't Repeat Yourself

Exercises

PROBLEM:
Given that the database is completely clean, write Python code that would create a user "Mike Stark" with email "subscribe@pythonvisually.com". Add "Toyota Prius" to her collection of cars.

YOUR CODE:

```
1
2
3
4
5
6
```

ANSWER:

```
cursor.execute('INSERT INTO users VALUES(NULL, '
                '"subscribe@pythonvisually.com", "Mike Stark")')
cursor.execute('INSERT INTO cars VALUES(NULL, "Toyota", "Prius", 1)')
```

Exercises

PROBLEM:
Write an SQL command that would let you remove any car produced by Ford.

YOUR CODE:
```
1
2
3
4
5
6
```

ANSWER:
```
1.  DELETE FROM cars WHERE brand = "Ford"
```

Exercises

PROBLEM: Write an SQL command to remove every car owned by user #17.

YOUR CODE:

```
1
2
3
4
5
6
```

ANSWER:

```
1.  DELETE FROM cars WHERE owner = 17
```

123

Part III: Popular 3rd party libraries

3rd party packages

Aside from the default Python packages, there are a variety of 3rd party solutions.
In order to use them in a similar fashion as the standard library they must be placed under PYTHONPATH.
PYTHONPATH is an environment variable that tells the interpreter where to look for Python source files.

The standard way to install Python packages is to use "pip", which has a simple command line interface.This is how to install:

https://pip.pypa.io/en/latest/installing.html

Find all packages that have a "nose" string in their name:

```
pip search nose
```

Install a package named "nose":

```
pip install nose
```

Show information about the "nose" package.

```
pip show nose
```

Get rid of the nose package:

```
pip uninstall nose
```

Web Development with Flask

Python can be a great choice when it comes to creating websites, and there are a lot of frameworks out there to help you with this task. This chapter provides an overview of one of them, Flask (http://flask.pocoo.org/), which is very easy to get started with.

Flask is a microframework, it keeps its core simple but extensible. The base framework is intended to be very lightweight, while new features can be added through extensions. Core features are:

> built in development server and debugger

> integrated unit testing support

> heavily uses HTTP methods

> uses Jinja2 templating

> supports secure cookies

> 100% WSGI 1.0 compliant

> unicode based

> extensively tested and documented

To begin with, install the framework:

```
pip install flask
```

Create a file name hello.py with the following code:

```
pip install flask
from flask import Flask
```

```
1.  app = Flask(__name__)
2.
3.  @app.route("/")
4.  def hello():
5.      return "Hello World!"
6.
7.  if __name__ == "__main__":
8.      app.run(debug = True)
```

and run it:

```
python hello.py
```

If you open your web browser and type:

http://localhost:5000

you should be greeted with the warming sight of "Hello World!"

Congratulations, you have just created your first website with Flask.

Let's walk through hello.py line by line.

1. First, the Flask class is imported from the flask module.
2. Then, an instance of the Flask class called app is created.
3. `@app.route("/")` tells Flask the URL that will trigger the method below it.
4. The `hello()` method is defined, which returns the string "Hello World!"
5. app.run starts the HTTP server.

Hello World

Create a new file called test.py:

```
1.  from flask import Flask
2.
3.  app = Flask(__name__)
4.
5.  @app.route("/")
6.  def root():
7.      return "Request Path is: " + request.path
8.
9.  @app.route("/test/")
10. def test():
11.     return "Request Path is " + request.path
12.
13. if __name__ == "__main__":
14.   app.run(debug = True)
```

You can see that a request module was imported from flask. This object represents an HTTP request sent by the client and received by the server, which contains the path of the requested page, the type of the request, and other information about the client and the transmitted data.

In this case, you have used the request object to return the path of the page.

Flask offers an easy way to answer to different HTTP methods:

```
1.  @app.route("/data", methods=['GET'])
2.  def show_data():
3.      ....
4.
5.  @app.route("/data", methods=['POST'])
6.  def handle_data():
7.      ....
```

Hello World

```
1.  @app.route("/user/<username>")
2.  def greet_user(username):
3.      return "Hello " + username
```

You can use sections of the webpage's URL as a variable in your function.

```
1.  import json
2.
3.  from flask import make_response, Flask
4.
5.
6.  app = Flask(__name__)
7.
8.
9.  @app.route("/json")
10. def get_image():
11.     # Create response
12.     response = make_response(json.dumps({"foo": "bar"}))
13.     # Set correct mimetype
14.     response.mimetype = "application/json"
15.     return response
16.
17.
18. if __name__ == "__main__":
19.     app.run(debug = True)
```

Until now, all of the pages would return simple text. Flask would automatically transform this string into an HTTP response, and would give it the mimetype "text/html" along with a status code 200. Now let's modify this behavior.

This code returns a JSON object.

We can also change the error code:

```
1.  ...
2.
3.  @app.route("/error")
4.  def error_page():
5.      response = make_response("Error Page")
6.      response.status_code = 404
7.      return response
8.
9.  ...
```

Quiz

PROBLEM:

1. What is Flask and what should you use it for?

2. Why is Flask called a microframework?

3. What is the default port for the Flask integrated HTTP server?

4. Can you cite most frequently used HTTP methods?

5. Consider the following code snippet:

```
1.  @app.route("/error")
2.  def error_page():
3.      return "Error Page"
```

ANSWER:

1. Flask is a microframework for Python used to create web applications.

2. It keeps its core simple. New functionality must be added via extensions.

3. 5000

4. *GET*, *POST*, *HEAD*, *PUT* and *DELETE*

5. 200. Do not be fooled by the error name. You did nothing to change the status code.

Exercises

PROBLEM:

Imagine you want to create a small discussion page for your website to let your users post and read messages. Messages are sorted in descending order, so the most recent message is displayed first.

Your website is so popular that soon there are too many messages to be displayed! You decide to limit the number of messages per page to 50, and add "next" and "previous" buttons to navigate between pages.

Can you create a script to display the first and last post number on a given page?

SAMPLE ANSWER

```
1.  ...
2.
3.  @app.route("/posts")
4.  @app.route("/posts/page/<int:page_nb>")
5.  def show_posts(page_nb = 1):
6.      first_msg = 1 + 50 * (page_nb 1)
7.      last_msg = first_msg + 49
8.      return "Messages {} to {}".format(first_msg, last_msg)
9.
10. ...
```

NOTES:

> set a default value for the variable page_nb so that the routes "/posts" and "/posts/page/1" are equivalent.

> force page_nb to be of type int int the decorator.
> So that a route "/posts/page/something" would return a 404 error.

131

Recipes for task automation

Working with files and directories can rapidly grow into a tedious and time consuming task. Python offers convenient methods to help you easily walk directories and perform operations on files.

The following code will scan all directories and subdirectories in a topdown manner:

```python
1.  import os
2.
3.  for root, dirs, files in os.walk(".",
    topdown = True):
4.      for name in files:
5.          print(os.path.join(root, name))
6.      for name in dirs:
7.          print(os.path.join(root, name))
```

Slate is a small module you can use to easily extract text from PDF files.

The following code reads a PDF file and extracts all text from the document, presenting each page as a string of text:

```python
>>> import slate
>>> f = open("doc.pdf")
>>> doc = slate.PDF(f)
>>> doc
[..., ..., ...]
>>> doc[1]
"Text from page 2...."
```

Python makes it easy to access remote resources using the urllib.

```python
>>> from urllib.request import urlopen
>>> response = urlopen("http://a/b/c")
>>> data = response.read()
```

Note that "response" is a file-like object, which points at the remote resource.

133

Image Processing

The Python Imaging Library (PIL) adds image processing capabilities to Python. You can use this library to create thumbnails, convert between file formats, print images, etc.

Load image from a file:

```
>>> import Image
>>> im = Image.open("Python.jpg")
```

Get a list of pixels from the image opened above:

```
>>> data = list(im.getdata())
```

The script below downloads a picture from a given url, rotates it, resizes it, and saves it locally.

```
1.  from PIL import Image
2.  from urllib.request import urlopen
3.  import io
4.  response = urlopen("http://a/b/c.jpg")
5.  im_file = io.BytesIO(response.read())
6.  im = Image.open(im_file)
7.  im = im.rotate(90)
8.  im = im.resize((800, 600))
9.  im.save("downloaded_image.jpg", "JPEG")
```

Note, io.BytesIO is used to wrap the buffer into a proper file-like object.

The following code creates a 128x128 thumbnail from a JPEG image:

```
1.  from PIL import Image
2.
3.  size = 128, 128
4.  filename = "image.jpg"
5.  im = Image.open(filename)
6.  im.thumbnail(size, Image.ANTIALIAS)
7.  im.save(filename + ".thumbnail", "JPEG")
```

Let's imagine that you need to clean up a directory and remove all files from before 2002. Each file within this directory is a text document (.txt) whose first line is a date (yyyy-mm-dd).

```python
1.  import os
2.  import time
3.
4.  count = 0
5.  kept = 0
6.  deleted = 0
7.  for (root, dirs, files) in os.walk('.'):for filename in files:
8.      if filename.endswith('.txt'):
9.          f = open(filename, 'r')
10.         sdate = f.readline();
11.         f.close()
12.         pdate = time.strptime(sdate, '%Y%-m%-d\n')
13.         if pdate.tm_year > 2002:
14.             kept += 1
15.         else:
16.             os.remove(filename)
17.         deleted += 1
18.     count += 1
19.
20. print('Total files: ' + str(count))
21. print('Kept: ' + str(kept))
22. print('Deleted: ' + str(deleted))
```

The code above does the following 4 things:

1. Imports the necessary modules.

2. Uses the "walk" method to navigate the current directory.For each text file in our directory a. Open file b. Read date using *f.readline()* c. Convert string date into Python object d. If date is before 2002 the file is deleted

3. For each text file in the directory:
    a. Open the file.
    b. Read the date using f.readline().
    c. Convert the date from a string to a Python object.
    d. Delete the file if the date is before 2002.

4. Keep count of the number of deleted files and display this number at the end.

135

Quiz

PROBLEM:

Why and when would you want to automate a task?

If *doc1.pdf* is a PDF document whose first page is blank, what does the following code print out?

```python
1.  import slate
2.  f = open("doc1.pdf")
3.  doc = slate.PDF(f)
4.  f.close()
5.  print(doc[0])
```

ANSWER:

1. Every time you need to do something over and over again, you may want to think of a way to automate this task to save yourself some time and make your life easier.

2. \n\n